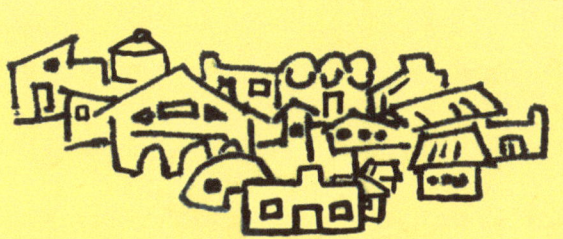

Rancho Linda Vista
Community of the Arts
Oracle, Arizona

1968
2018
50 Years
of Art and Living

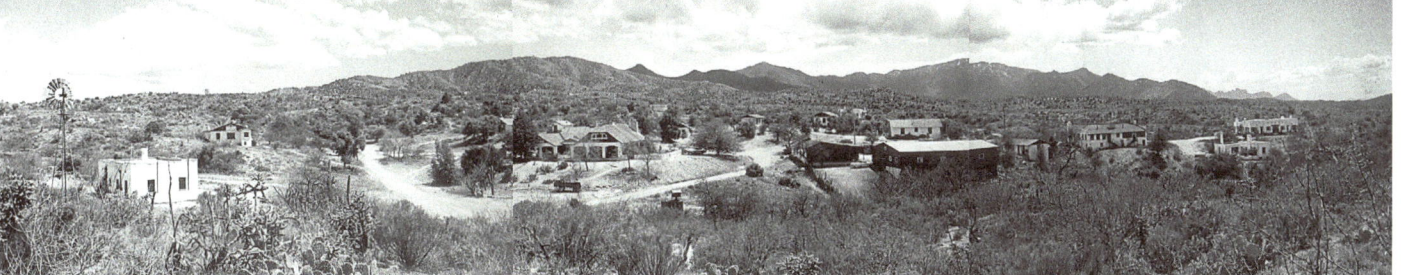

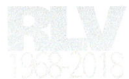
Timeline: Southern Arizona and Oracle

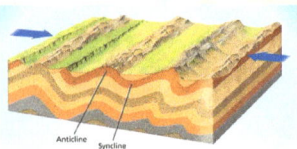

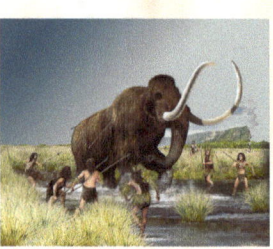

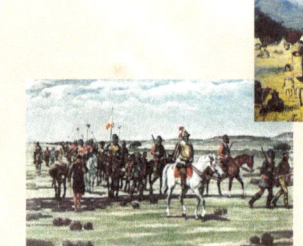

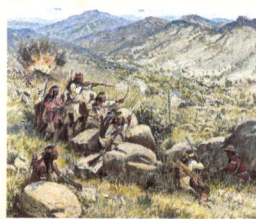

Mammoth hunters
11–13,000 years ago

First Spaniards & horses
1540
Apaches enter Southern Arizona
1540–1690

Santa Catalina Mountains formed
35 million years ago

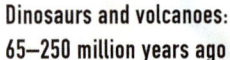

The Hohokam
700s–1450

Apache Wars
1870s

Dinosaurs and volcanoes:
65–250 million years ago

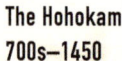

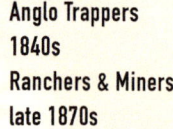

Anglo Trappers
1840s
Ranchers & Miners
late 1870s

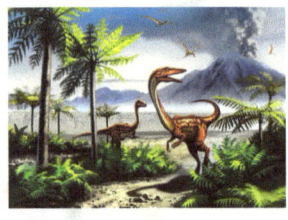

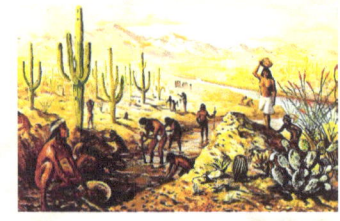

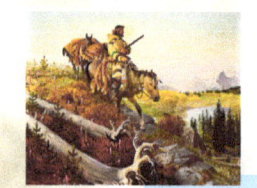

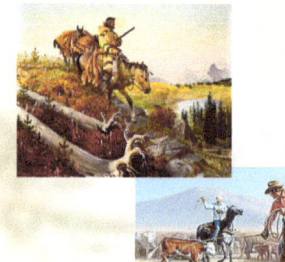

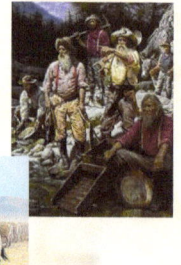

"When someone writes the history
of the Ranch, it will be fiction."

—*Marilyn Nelson*

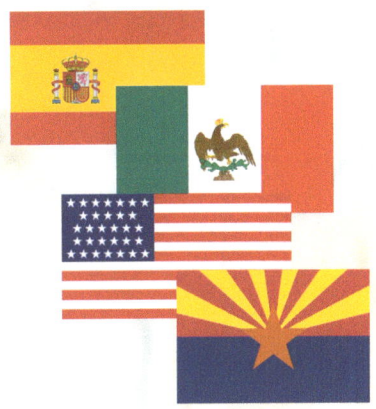

History

Rancho Linda Vista is situated at 4500 feet in the northern foothills of the Santa Catalina mountains which separate it from the city of Tucson 35 miles away. Starting as a homestead around the turn of the century, it developed into a large cattle-ranch that later evolved into a well-known guest ranch.

In 1968 the Ranch buildings and 80 acres were bought by a group of people mostly connected with the arts who were interested in exploring other ways of living than they had yet found possible in an urban setting. In 1975 the Ranch incorporated for the stated purpose of providing and maintaining an environment in which artistic endeavors and related activities could flourish.

Today the Ranch enjoys a mutually satisfying relationship with the nearby small town of Oracle. It is a leader in artistic activities of a professional nature and our residents, which number about 25 adults and 20 children, take part in local affairs. We have had a member on the school board, members on various committees, and our children attend the local schools.

Arizona "belonged" to:
Spain to 1821
Mexico to 1853
US Territory to 1912
Statehood 1912

Rancho Linda Vista established
as arts community
1968

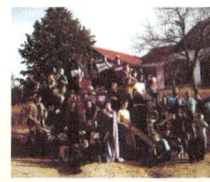

Oracle Post Office
established
1880

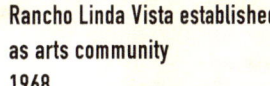

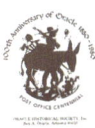
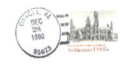

Wilson Ranch
1911
Rancho Linda Vista Guest Ranch
1924 – 1951
Wilson Barn built 1957
Tres Amigos own RLV
1957–1968

Tom Wilson dies
1994
Wilson Ranch acreage
sold off for development

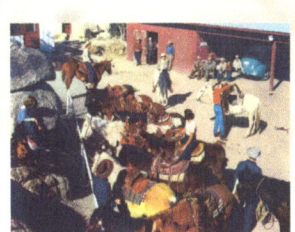

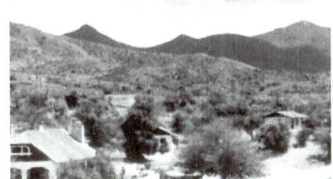

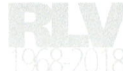

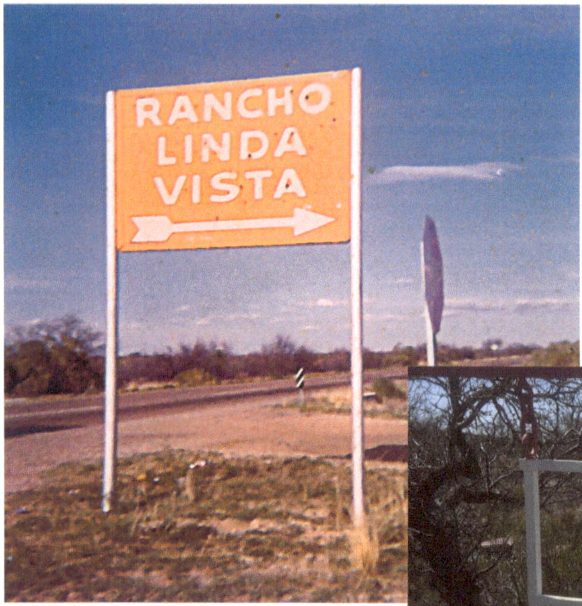

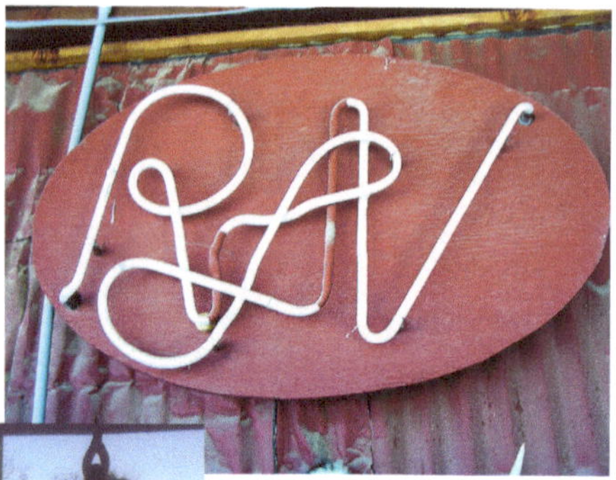

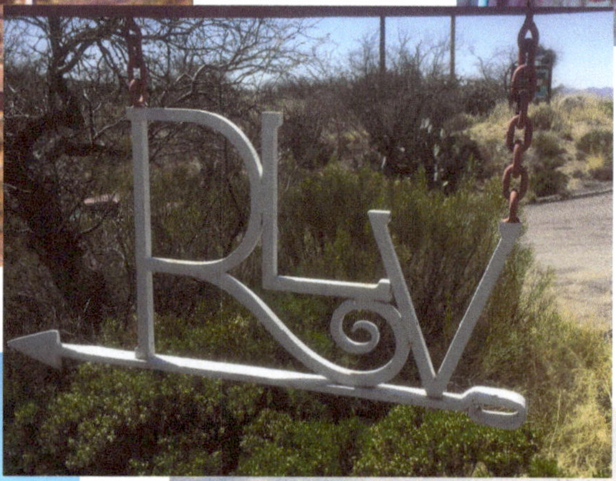

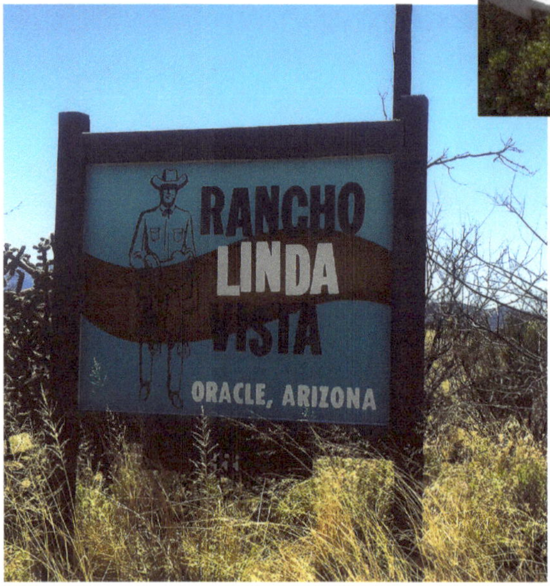

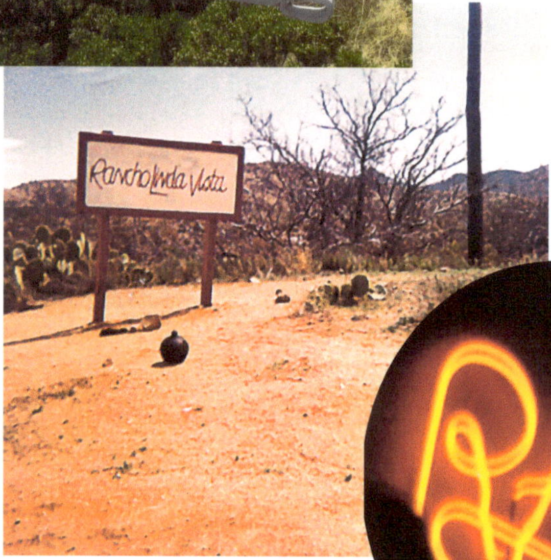

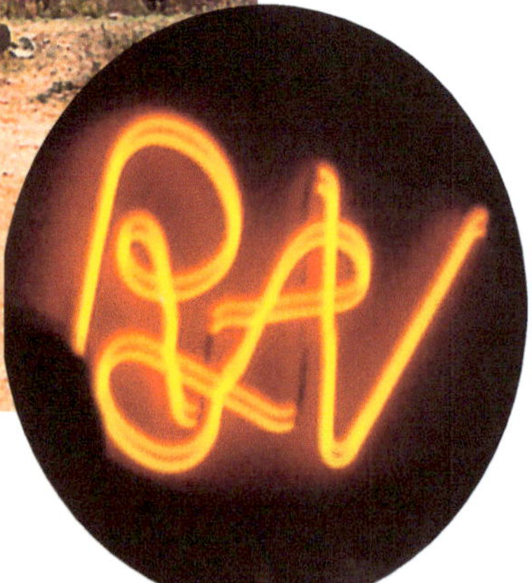

January 1968

Monday: *Ivy and I visit Charles. He shows me an ad for a place called Rancho Linda Vista...*

Friday: *Charles has been talking to people all week about the ranch. I am beginning to hear names I never heard before...*

Saturday: *It is bright. I stop at Charles'. We talk about people to be called, sandwiches to make...*

Sunday: *It is windy, sunny. Charles is tight with excitement. Somebody is wearing wooden shoes. We feel like we are about to do something we like doing. There are many children and our cars tell us who we are before we do... At the ranch it is windier, sunnier. The windmill turns and turns. We meet the owners and get the keys. Then up the hill and into houses. They are filled with light and I think how much more is waiting to get in behind the plastic curtains. Some houses have pink wicker furniture like they had in church camp. The big kids run everywhere. The ground is soft and rich and the wash is glistening. We sit on a hill. We eat; we talk. Everybody talks. Sometimes we stand up when we talk, sometimes we are on our knees when we talk. The kids whisper to each other and whisper to their mothers, "Can we live here?" ... I look around. None of us look alike, dress alike ... we find we really don't know anything ... except that we want to live there, in this place, and yes, even with each other... The sun goes down. We go home.*

Thursday: *It rains all day... We have found the money for the down payment for Rancho Linda Vista and the life she holds for us.*

—Artis Schroeder

We were looking for a place were we could live among friends, a place that would be conducive to artists, and a place we felt comfortable raising our kids. We found Rancho Linda Vista.

—Charles Littler, quoted in *The Arizona Republic*, 1982

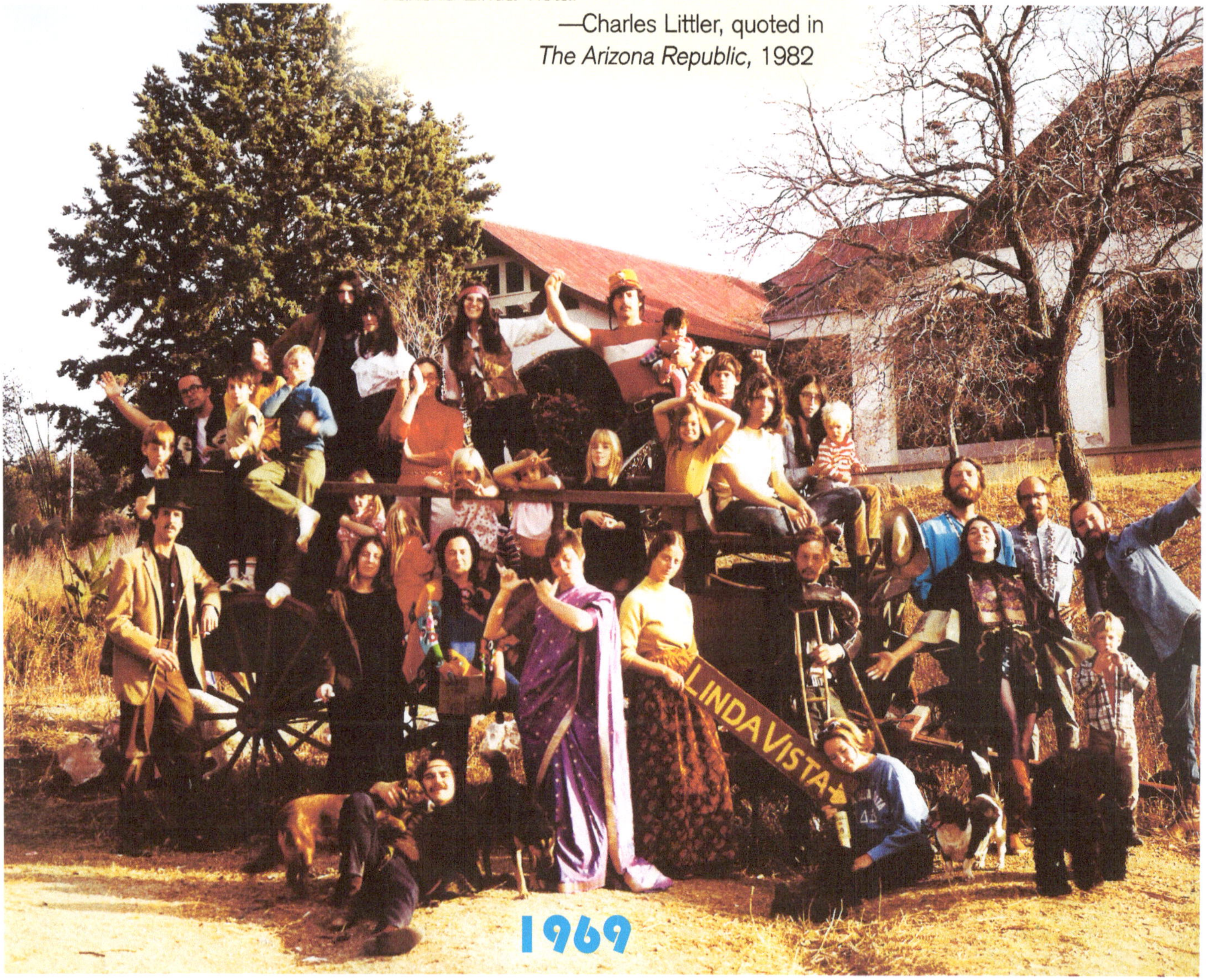

1969

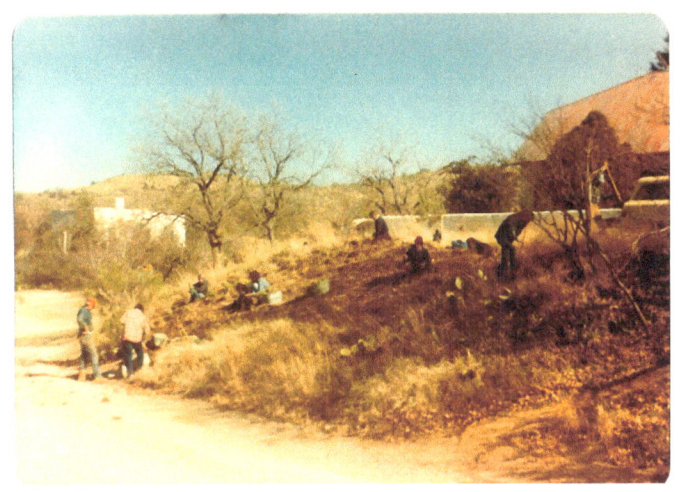
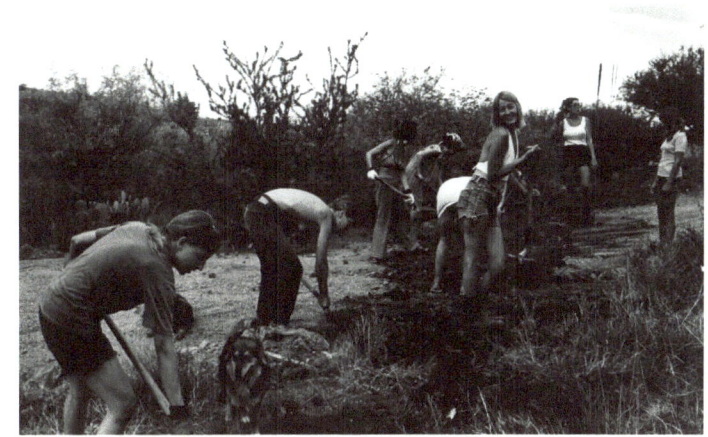

For all is not culture at Rancho Linda
Vista. Residents maintain the property
cooperatively. A paint brush must be sometimes set aside to push wheelbarrows of
dirt away from a cistern being built,
or to lay bricks in the floor of an old
studio-barn or to install a pane of glass.

[Jay Hall, Tucson Citizen, June 14, 1969]

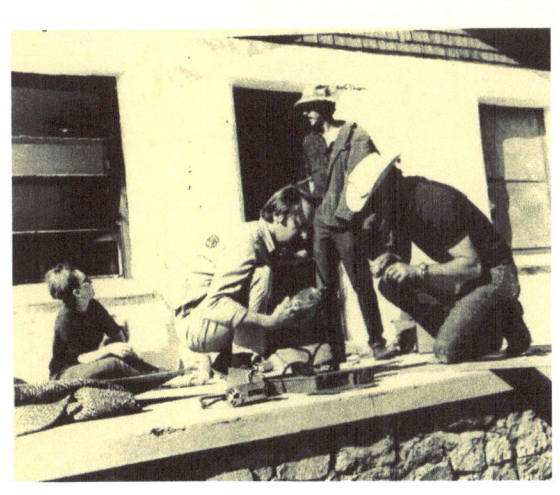
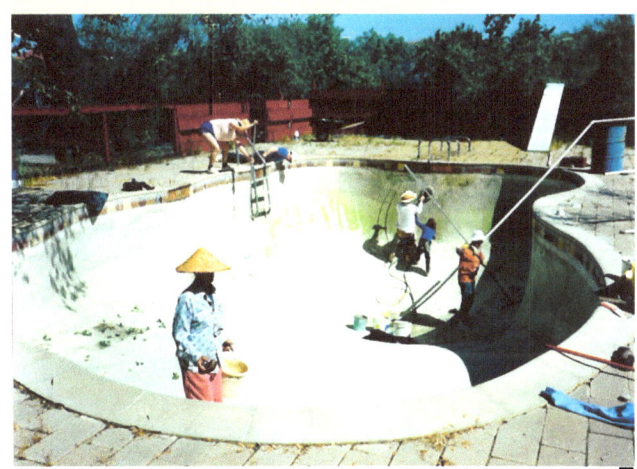

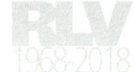

It happened in 1968.

- **Pueblo Incident**
- **Tet Offensive**
- **Prague Spring**
- **US Civil Rights** Movement
- **Student protests in France, US, Mexico, Poland**
- **Mr Rogers' Neighborhood**
- **My Lai massacre**
- **Martin Luther King assassinated**
- **Civil Rights Act**
- **Hair** "This is the dawning of the Age of Aquarius"
- **Biafra crisis**
- **Robert Kennedy assassinated**
- **Soviets invade Czechoslovakia**
- **Democratic National Convention in Chicago– riots, Chicago 7 trial, Yippies**
- **2001: A Space Odyssey, Planet of the Apes, Rosemary's Baby**
- **Northern Ireland: The Troubles**
- **Black power salute by US black medal winners at Mexico City Olympics**
- **Nixon elected President**
- White Album, Beggars Banquet
- Apollo 8 orbits moon; first photo of blue planet from space

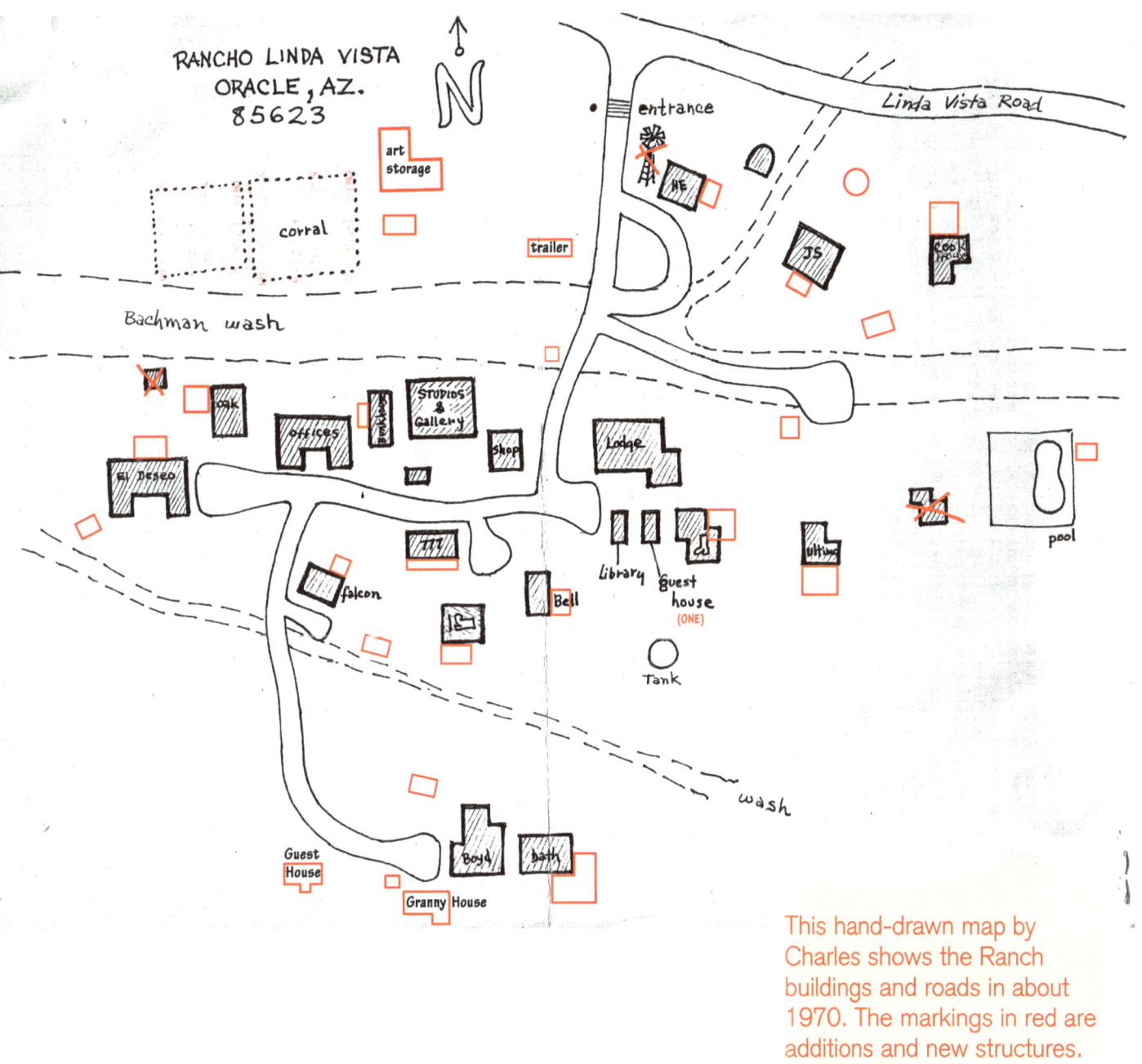

RANCHO LINDA VISTA
ORACLE, AZ.
85623

N

art storage

corral

trailer

Bachman wash

Linda Vista Road

entrance

RE

JS

COB

STUDIOS & Gallery

offices

pottery

Shop

oak

El Deseo

Lodge

falcon

library

guest house (ONE)

quilting

pool

Bell

Tank

wash

Boyd

bath

Guest House

Granny House

This hand-drawn map by Charles shows the Ranch buildings and roads in about 1970. The markings in red are additions and new structures.

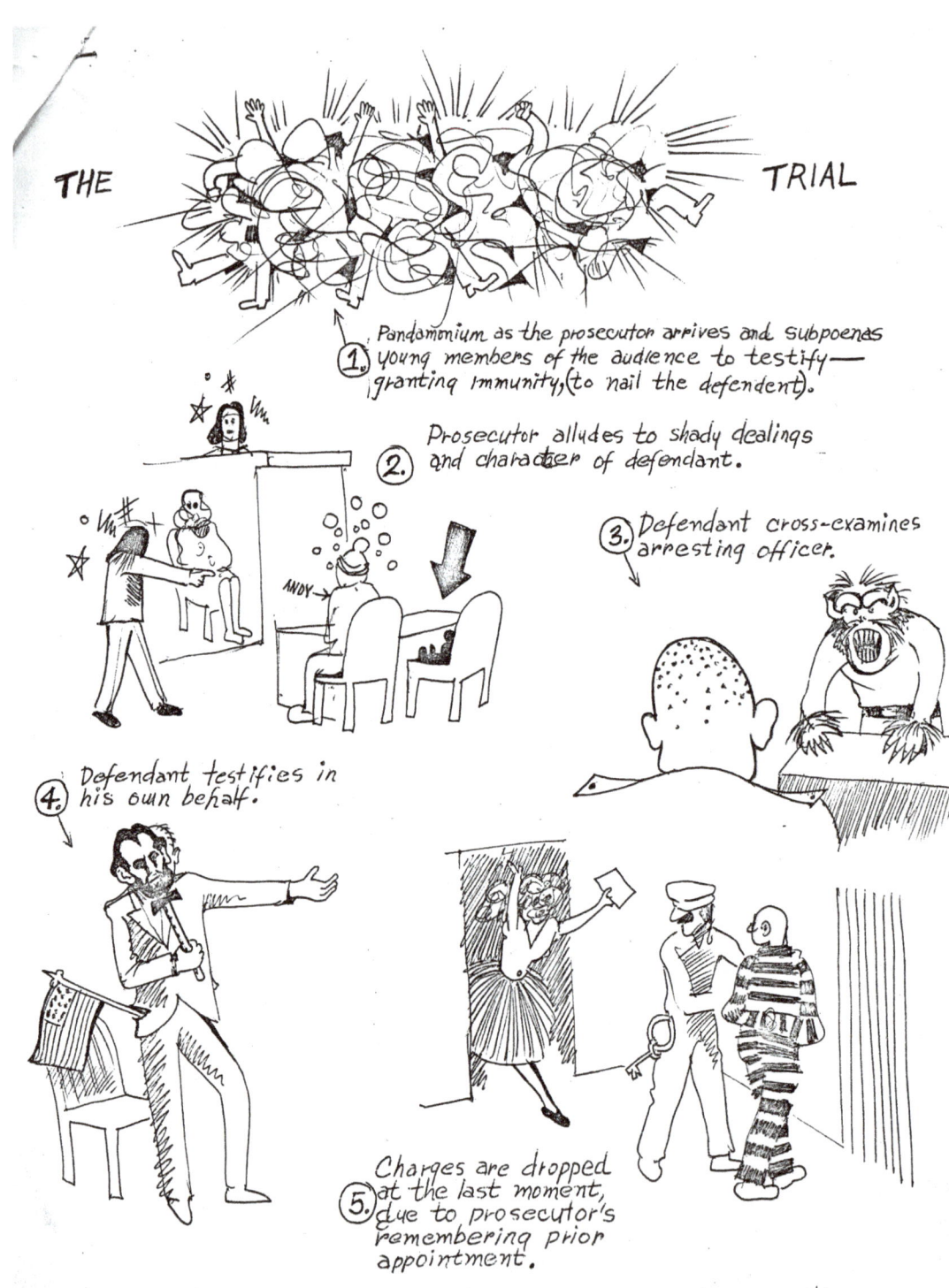

THE ... TRIAL

1. Pandamonium as the prosecutor arrives and subpoenas young members of the audience to testify—granting immunity, (to nail the defendant).

2. Prosecutor alludes to shady dealings and character of defendant.

3. Defendant cross-examines arresting officer.

ANDY

4. Defendant testifies in his own behalf.

5. Charges are dropped at the last moment, due to prosecutor's remembering prior appointment.

— Flash Littler

after the infamous Halloween Party raid. 1975

'Utopia' Isn't Coming True for Desert Group

[Kenneth Reich. LA Times, Feb 9, 1969]

Oracle, Ariz-- A modern drama of social striving for Utopia and bitter frustration in not finding it is being enacted near this small desert town.

The attempt of a group of University of Arizona instructors and Tucson professional people to form a utopian community at a former dude ranch has fallen into terrible, perhaps fatal, difficulty...

...

On the other hand, there remains determination on the part of many members to preserve the democratic structure wherein all decisions are taken by the community as a whole. Even the management committee has been relegated to unimportant status.

...

Littler said that when he and the others had moved into the Ranch last April they had "no knowledge how it would turn out or what we were getting into. We had a blind trust." What has happened since, he said, has been "illuminating and growth-producing."

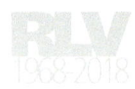

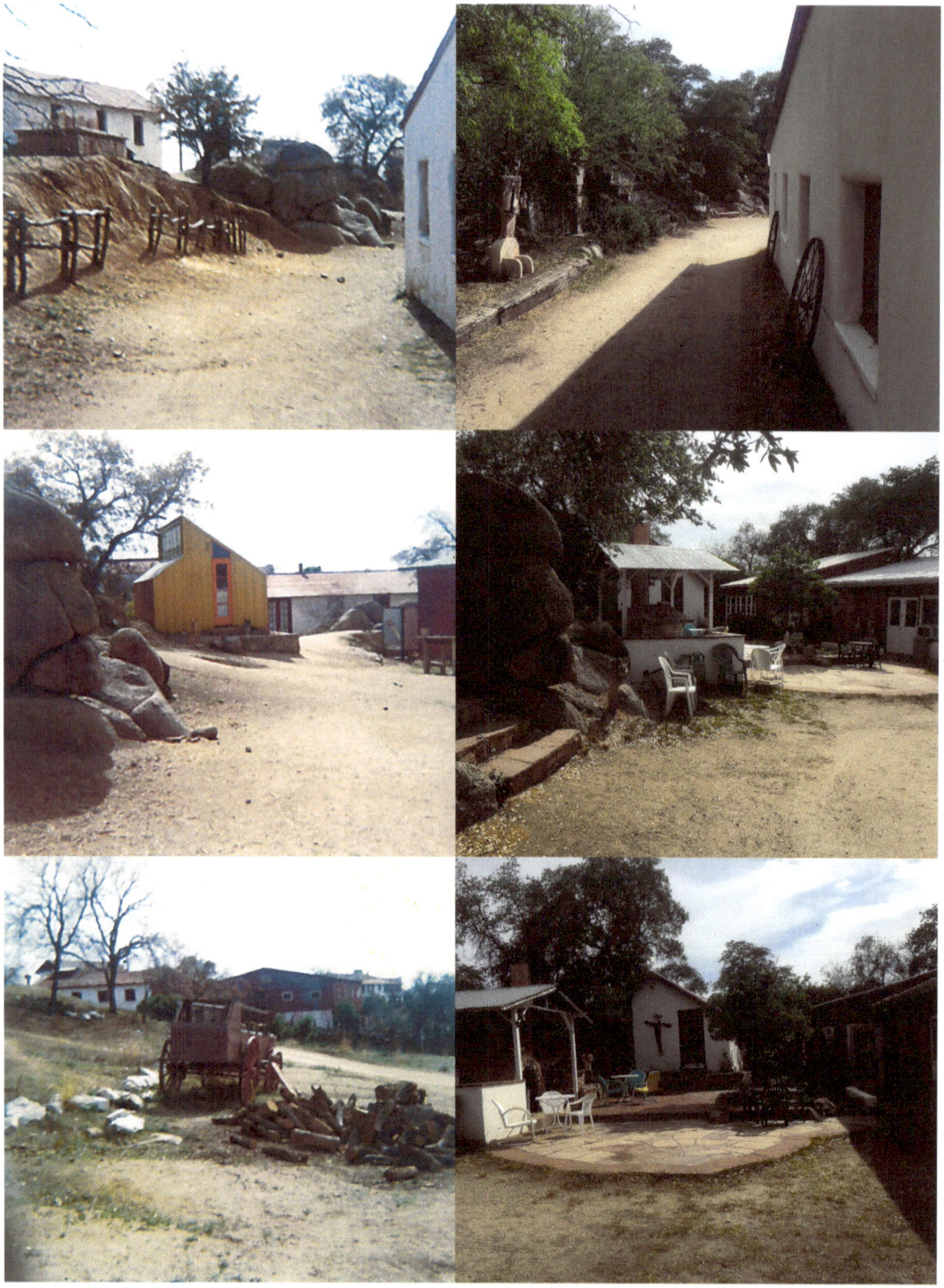

1968   2018

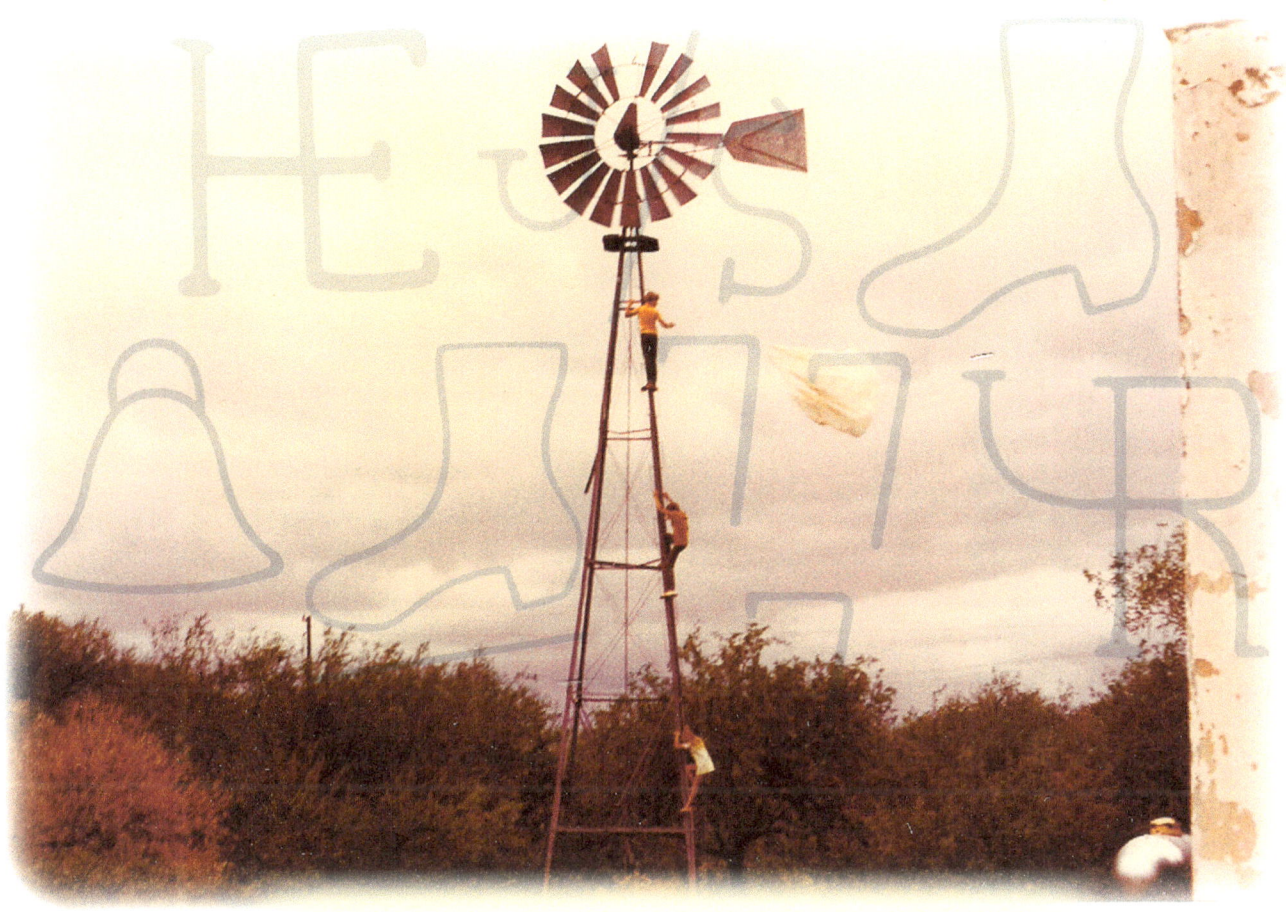

A Rumor*

overheard at an opening:

After Warhol came to RLV for the filming of "Lonesome Cowboys," he put in a bid on the property even though he knew the artist group who'd invited him there was already in the process of buying it. Said it would become the Factory West.

—*unattributed & unsubstantiated*

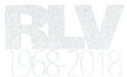
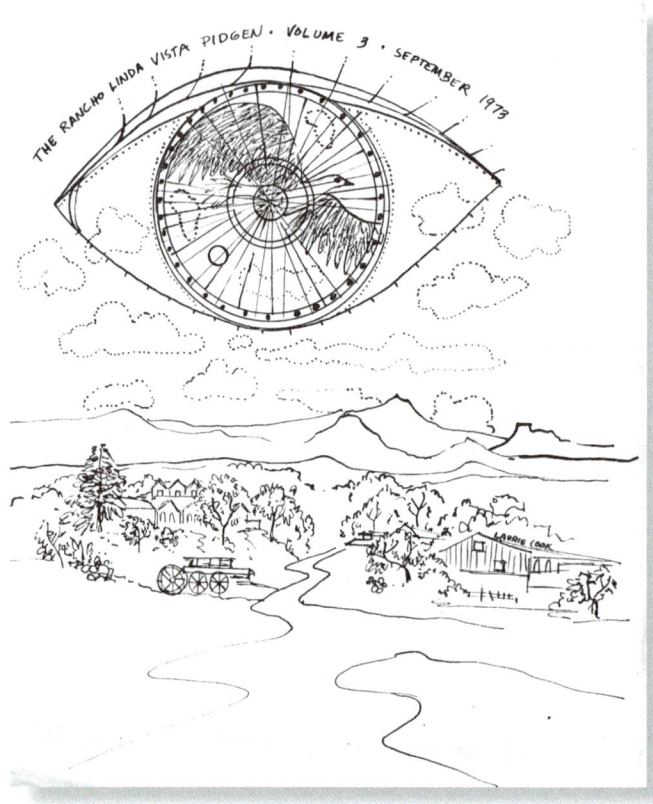

THE RANCHO LINDA VISTA PIDGEN · VOLUME 3 · SEPTEMBER 1973

The Pidgen—
edited by Charlotte,
Terry and others,
circa 1973–75.

Here are two covers
drawn by Laurie Cook.

WANT ADS and PERSONALS

Tarot Readings- Know the future if you dare-
call 896-2466
———————————
Arthur was right, there is a crab epidemic
in Tucson. -Jean
———————————
I want a lot. -charlotte
———————————
Anyone who has a game of Clue and interested
in same contact Marilyn or Arnie
———————————
Anyone who has old bricks to spare,
contact Fox
———————————
Needed and Wanted: someone who can draw a
decent pidgin for the cover of this damn
thing. Unsalaried position.
———————————
"Even the fun at the Ranch is heavy."
-visitor to the ranch

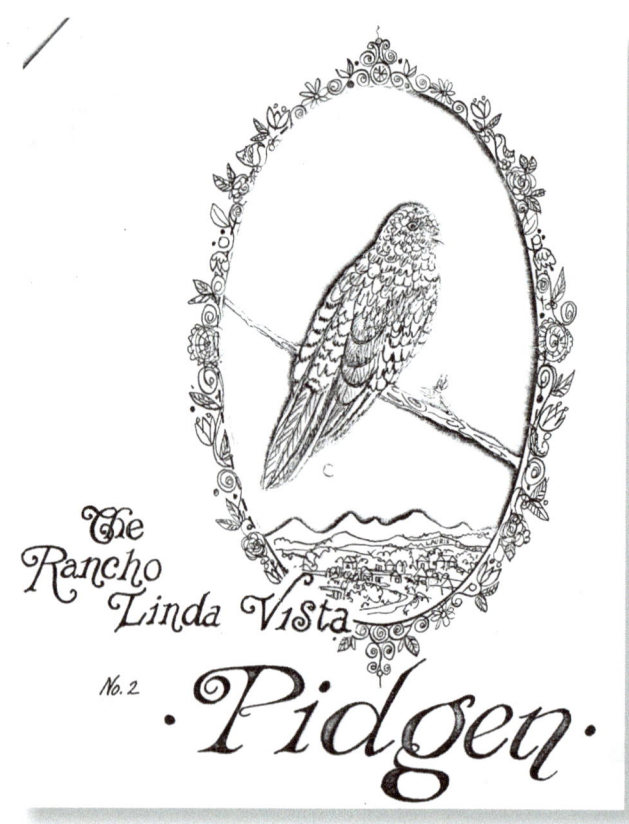

The Rancho Linda Vista No. 2 · Pidgen ·

The Fistfight

Laurie's VERSION

I hear a thud at the front door. It opens as if from a strong gust of wind. For me everything stops. Then slow motion. A tangle of arms and legs rolls across the carpet. I lean forward. I see a pair of hands go down, a shirt being jerked and ripped...
"...trying to beat me up."
Then Boyd is up and looking. He sits between Elli and me at the table.
"Are you alright?" we say in unison, touching him.
A pale face comes towards us, his arm outstretched, his mouth moving with apologies and hopes. He and Boyd begin to shake hands. A shadow of another young man jostles him then moves in closer to our table. And lifting his leg as if to piss, he leans his foot on its edge and shoves...
"Now wait a minute!"
Pitchers, cashew bags, glasses, cigarettes, money , slide past my lap onto the floor. A thin stream of beer turns back on itself as the table teeters upright.
"Now wait a minute!"   the table
Charles is up then pushed into, stomach first, arching over it to mid-top, arching back as if sprung from a trampoline, landing on his feet.
I feel my hand go to the table, my foot to the floor. I look up. A fist is coming towards me, in rapid three dimensions, followed by a face, his eyes pinched shut, his mouth puckered. I lean slightly to the side. I hear his fist, his arm go by my face, feel his body brush against me as he wheels back out into the room. Chris is in the circle of men, yelling. David stands up, removes his glasses, and hands them to me.
"Here, hold these for me."
He walks bent slightly forward out into the room. I see him from the back, his hands on Chris' shoulders. He is taller than the rest. There is much talking, louder.
"Lets get out of here"
I drop to the floor, searching for my wallet. I find a purse, yell purse, someone takes it.
"I need my glasses, Laurie." David's glasses are clutbhed tightly in my hand. I raise my arm. Our hands touch in midair. I consider leaving my wallet then think better of it. I am holding the edge of the table. The noise in the room is getting louder. I find my wallet only by its leather softness against the sharp edges of glass and soggy ashes on the floor. Someone hands me my coat. My keys are still in its pocket. I walk to the front door and take its wooden edge in my hand...
I am outside. Oracle. Bettys. The unlighted Exxon sign. The air is cool, the moon bright. I turn around. Someone has gone back in. We wait. Chris comes out.
"Let's go."
I start the motor...for once it doesn't stall. We share a pack of Camels. The dirt road feels good, headlights filter through the dust, the cattle guard rumbles beneath me. I stop the motor. We get out, circle the car. I climb Arthurs stairway of rubber and chipped white paint. I open another door. We are inside.
Charles builds a fire. I make hot chocolate. We sit on the floor and tell the story, over and over. A marshmallow foam touches my lips. My heart is fluttering and I am surprised. I try to calm it. It doesn't work. I have come home again.

                                        Laurie

CHRIS'S VERSION

CHRIS'S VERSION

Monday night after the Gallery meeting, Boyd, Laurie, Ellie, Pam, Charles Andy, Danvid Mod me went to the Oracle Inn and were having a wonderful time drinking, dancing and sharing. As the evening progressed the four men beside us got increasingly drunk and rowdy; making cracks at us and bumping the men when they would get up from their table. Ellie danced with the tall Mexican guy. Pam started to dance with the blond guy in a T-shirt but he then retorted that he couldn't dance with her, because he had no penecillin. She let the insult slide , muttering to us from time to time. The mood still remained hilarious, but not wit hou! an element of pressure. Boyd felt this intently and went outside. I heard the guy with the gimp, say to the guy in the T-shirt, to wait there until the time was right. I said to Laurie, that I was alarmed because I knew he was going outside to fight Boyd.
We agreed that they were evenly matched, and that he could hold his own. Time spaced by and I realized that there was only one man at the table. I began to be alarmed when the door burst open and in rolled Boyd, with 3 guys on top. He was bloody and down on his hands and knees. They were tearing at his T-shirt and enjoying themselves. I stood up and screamed "I saw you assholes go after him", and one man retorted " Yeah, well he's a queer". I was irate, Pam was in the middle of the saying "just tell me what has happened." Boyd was on his feet, so I was David and Charles. David was holding me back. The men were momentarily taken aback and stunned because they realized that they were dealing with the women. Then
The big, Mexican dude just started swinging and knocking things over (he was the one who punched Boyd). The bartender started to come from out of the bar and the big dude tackled him, laid him flat, turned around, pushed Pam (she hurt her nose), pushed Charles, who bounced back and said "Wait a minute, here". The big dude kicked our table over. David took a Tai-Chi stance and handed his glasses to Laurie. Andy was still sitting with glass and stuff flying all around him. He then picked up his coat and started handing other people's coats to them. The men started fighteing among themselves and we all calmly gathered our belongings; strewn everywhere) and filed out the door.
We sat in front of Laurie's fire, missing David and Andy, until one or two , rehashing the whole thing, and laughing. Charles fell asleep by the fire and woke up swinging. As of this morning, Tues., Boyd is finewith a swollen lip, the start of a black eye and a lot of felling inside for all of us and the whole incident.

                                        - Chris Hall

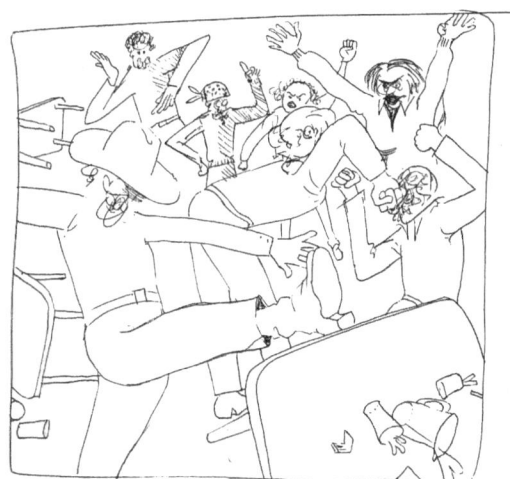

also from The Pidgen—
descriptions of an incident
at the Oracle Inn
(Laurie Cook, Chris Hall,
Flash Littler)

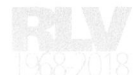

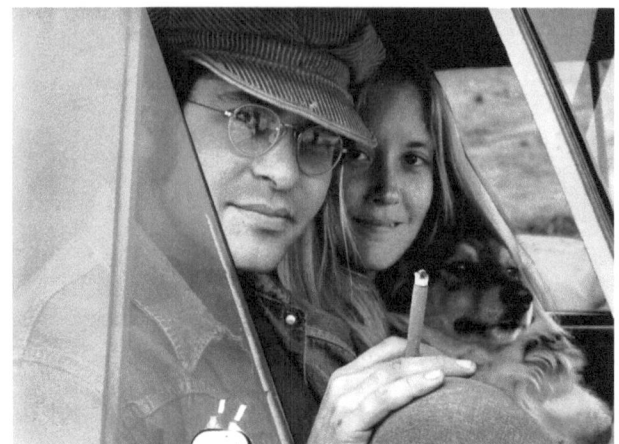

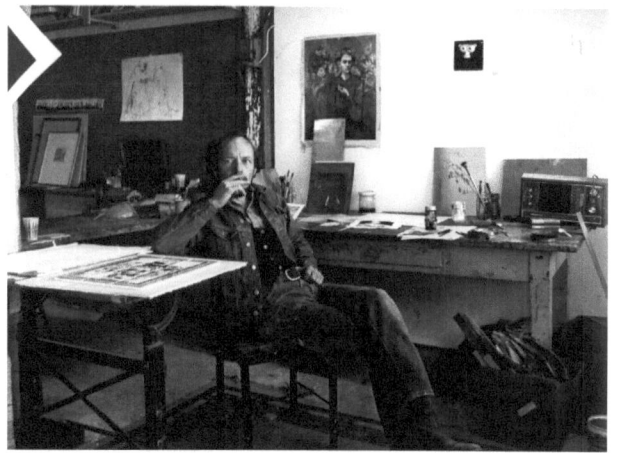

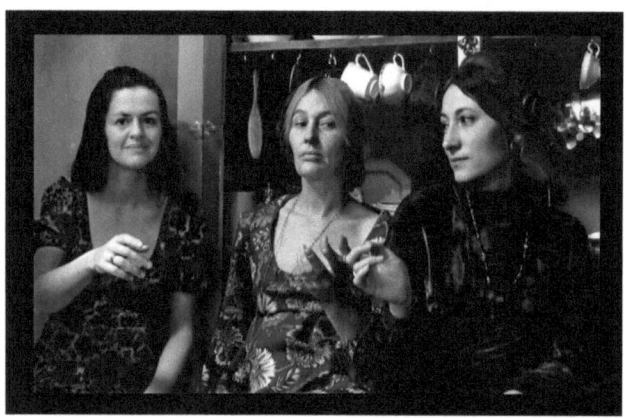

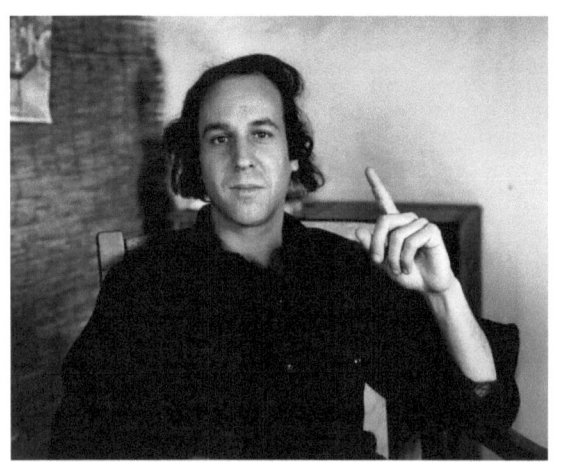

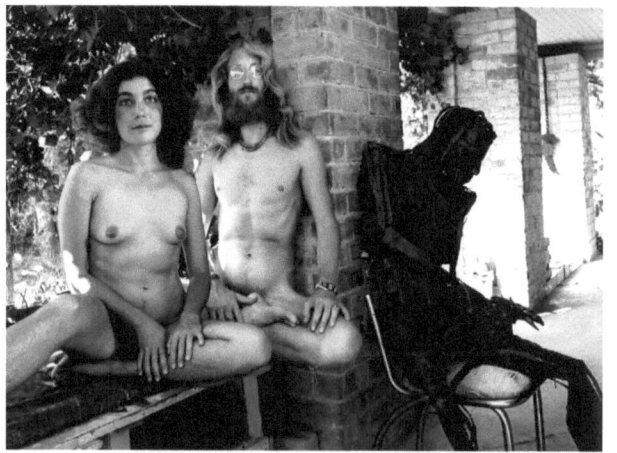

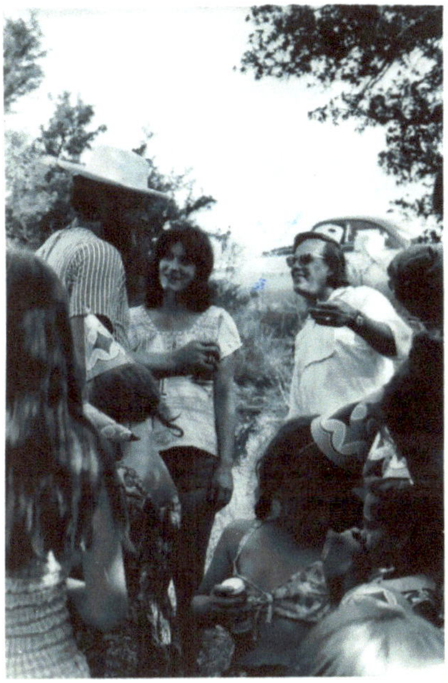

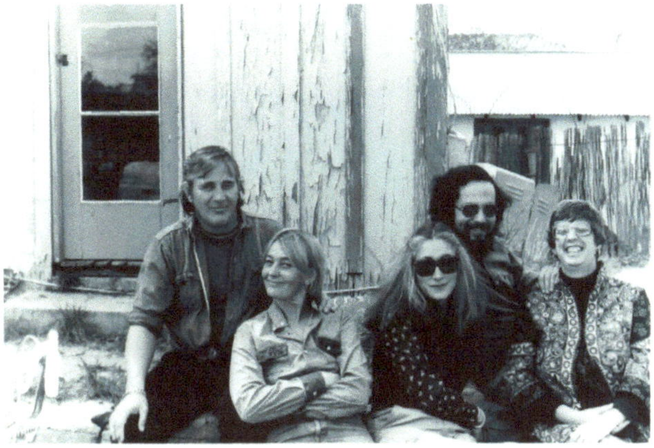

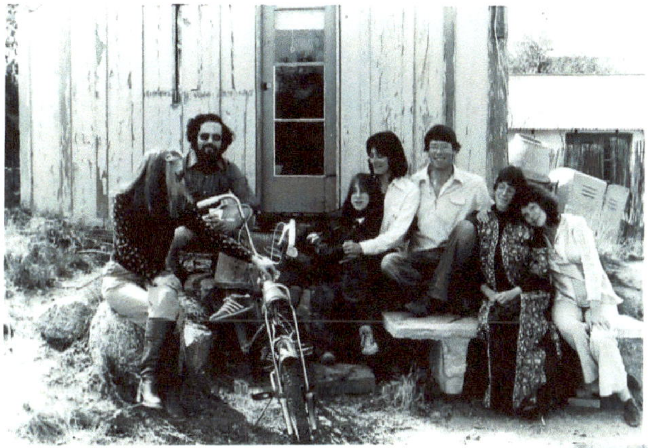

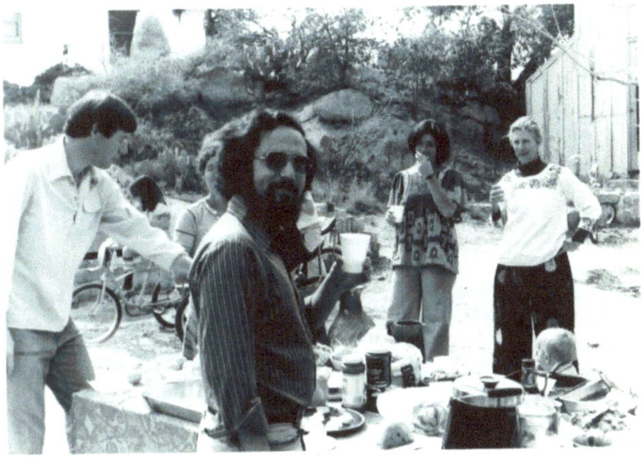

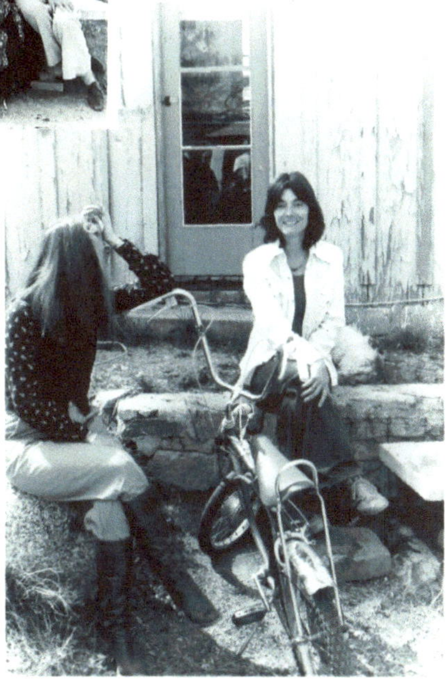

photos on this spread: Dana Slaymaker, c.1970

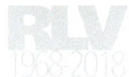

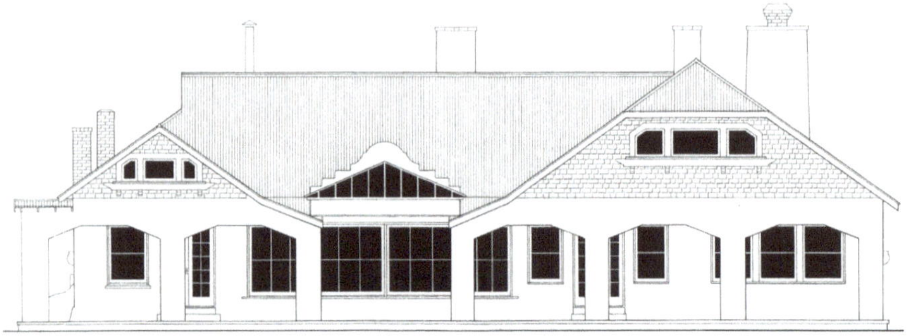

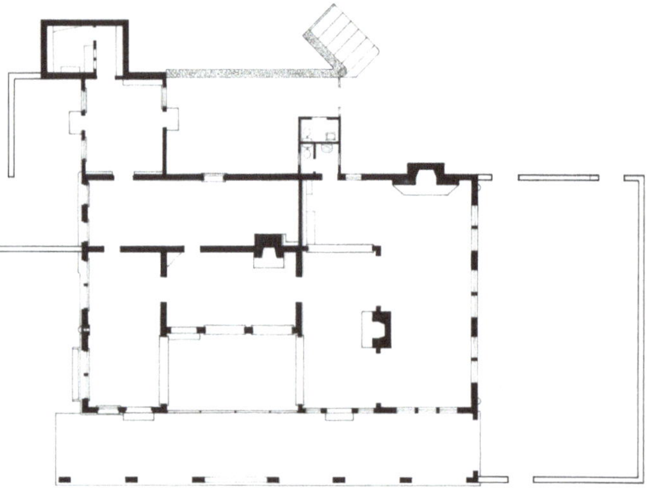

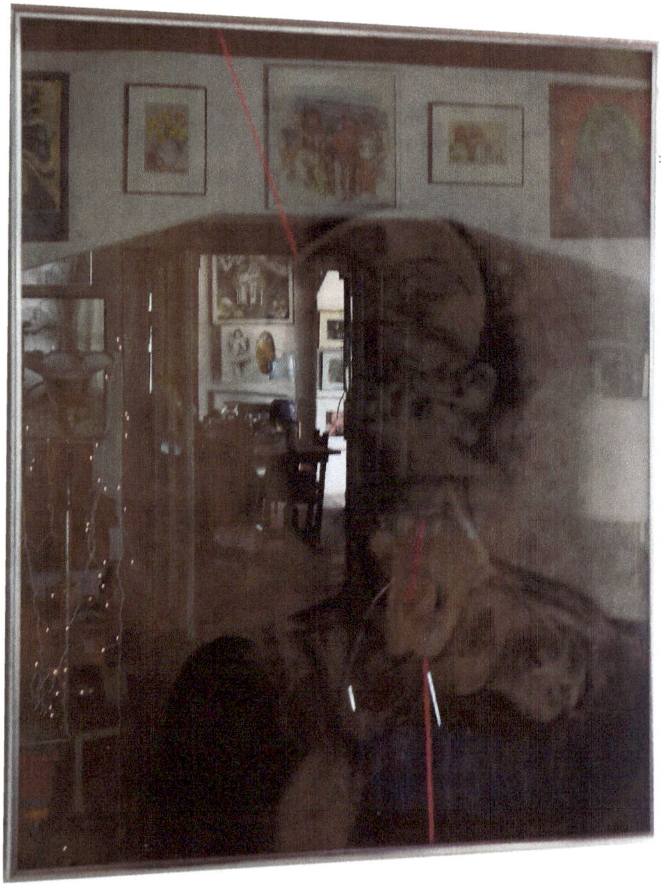

Chuck Sternberg architectural drawings of of The Lodge;
Charles Littler self-portrait reflecting the Nelson collection

A Moveable Feast at the Lodge — with apologies to Ernest Hemingway

There is never any ending to what the Lodge means to us and the memory of each person differs from that of any other. We found ourselves together there, no matter who was there or not there, or with what difficulties, or ease, it could be reached, intoxicated or sober. The Lodge was always coming home together and you received return for whatever you brought to it.

Bad chairs, good conversation

I spent a lot of time hanging out at the Lodge because the congenial Nelson family lived there and I lived alone. They made it easy to stop by and join in with anything going on. I spent so much time there I finally provided my own chair at the big round oak table in the kitchen—like having your own stein locker at the pub.

"If only you had a set of kitchen chairs with good backs, padded seats and arm rests, I wouldn't have to go home." The loose, hard wooden chairs often pinched my bare legs and became such a looming terror, that I donated chairs more suitable for frequent marathon sittings. I further colonized the Lodge by bringing over framed art-work, painted furniture and snack bowls to add to the ambience.

Lots of times I visited just Marilyn, mostly during the day to take a break from my work. She was the hearth, always welcoming and available, making her a generous hostess and deep friend. We'd have tea and talk. We spent a lot of time in the kitchen and in her sitting room watching the seasons pass and trading stories.

"Now that's dialogue!," shouted writer Alan Harrington when I first brought him to the Lodge kitchen. There were nearly ten of us sitting around with four or five conversations going on at once—art, politics, gossip, lots of laughter. There'd be drinks and snacks put out by Marilyn to fuel the flame—trail mix, pretzels, chocolate, coffee, tea, booze.

What could we have been talking about, visitors to the Lodge? — artists, painters, poets, writers, weavers, musicians, anthropologists, carpenters, builders, blacksmiths, sculptors, art dealers, collectors, curators, actors, directors, film makers, multi/mixed media artists, motorcyclists, watercolorists, potters, teachers, students, doctors, nurses, midwives, historians, engineers, sailors, scientists, journalists, cowboys, psychologists, programmers, priests, smokers, drinkers, drug-takers, eaters, mothers, fathers, sons, daughters, husbands, wives, companions, lovers, and friends.

Dreaming of the Lodge

The only time I remember sleeping in the Lodge was last spring. I felt lucky to spend the night there in Marilyn and Arnold's bed, though those dear friends were elsewhere, Arnold out of town, Marilyn in her Tucson home, burdened with Parkinson's and caretakers. The lilac bushes were blooming on the shady north side off the screened porch. As I drifted into sleep, crickets singing, I felt the history of events in the big house—parties, conversations, lives lived. I'd come home to sleep in the well of my dreams.

—*Margo Burwell, April 2018*

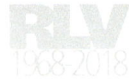

*portraits of Marilyn by
Jim Davis, Peggy Doogan,
Bruce McGrew, Charles Littler,
Andy Rush*

across: Arnold by Jim Davis

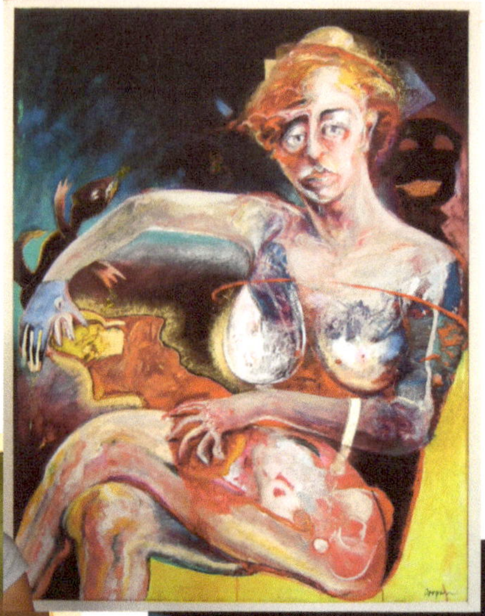

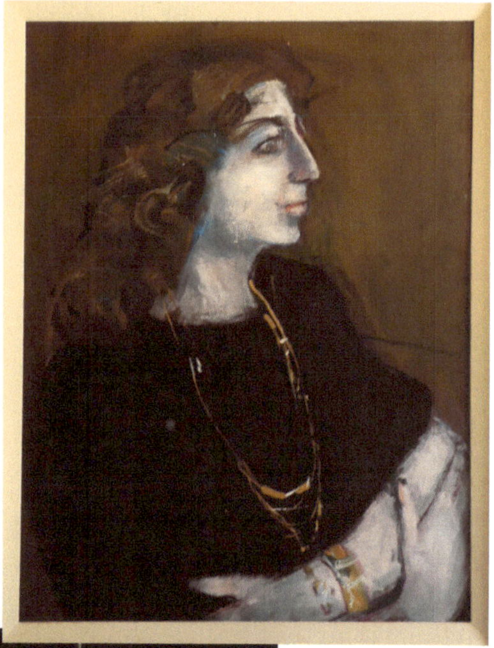

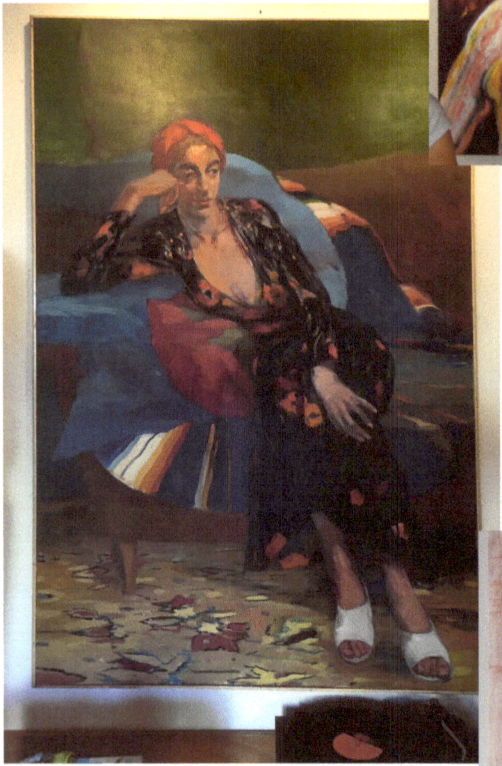

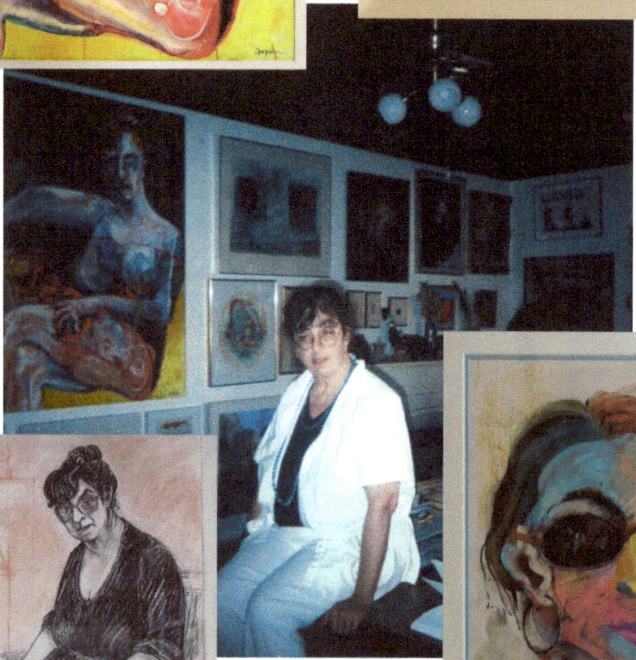

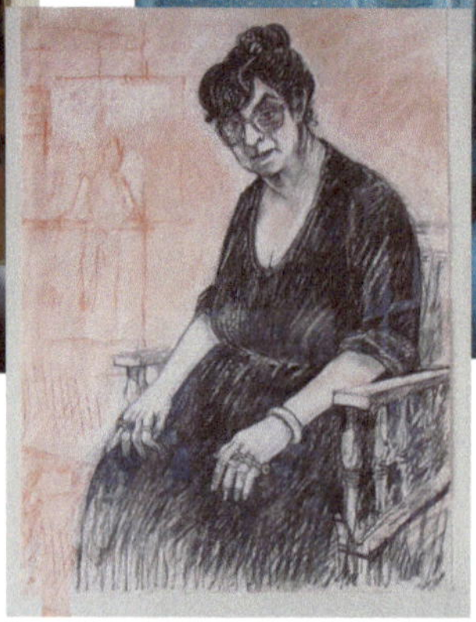

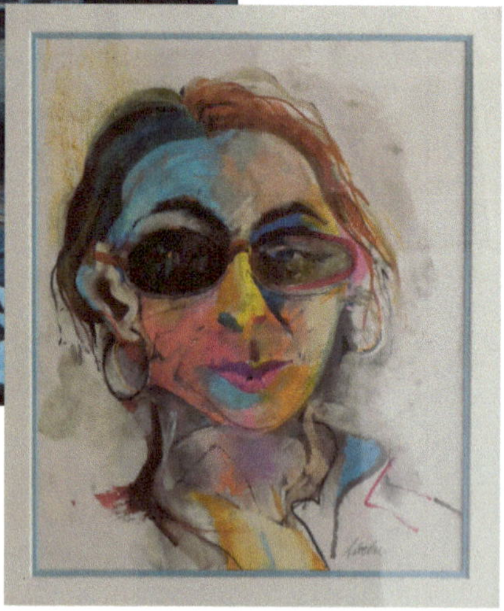

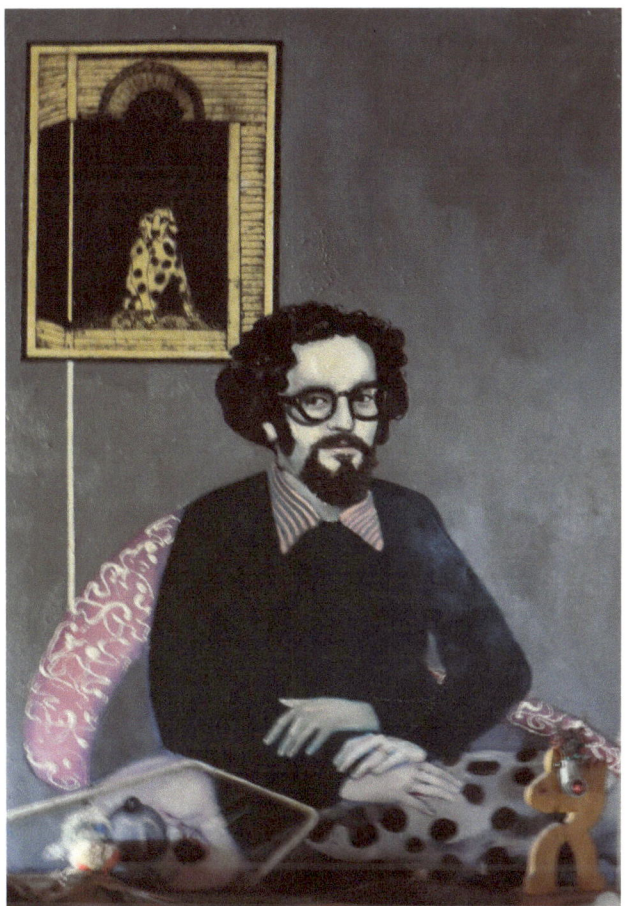

I think the year was 1984. Arnold and Marilyn commissioned me to design the divider;
 Davis's portrait was hanging on the wall right next to the divider opening. Now I have
 to say that I in those days I admired but was a little afraid of Jim--I'm an introvert--but
 I wanted to have a "dialog" with him in terms of his painting. As we all know, in the
 painting Arnold has three hands in his lap. So although my glass was appropriately
 abstract, incorporating the blue translucent edges of glass shelves into design, I decided
 to add some sand blast carved "floating" hands into the glass--and one of them is
 pointing straight at the hands in the portrait. so I was giving Jim The Big Wave with
 my glass hands.

—Mary Myers

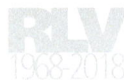
[Arnold Nelson speaking]

I'm going to give a spiel about this painting here—I've done this about a hundred times—I've even given it when the artist has been here, and he, like, gapes at me. This painting is called 'The Picnic' and it's by Jim Davis. Jim is what I call an expressionistic psychological narrative painter. This illustrates, sort of tells a story, and again, his theme, well—someone once called Jim the 'poet of creepiness.' On the surface, when you look at this piece, it's the American family at a picnic, and what could be more tranquil and lovely? Here they are in this beautiful setting, and everything is cool, but then you start to look at it more closely, and—I like to start with the man's face—he looks glazed, like he's been narcotized. He's not present. And the same thing with the woman's face. She's sort of out of it, too, but in contrast to the boy's face—the boy is alarmed. Something he's watching is making his mouth go into an 'O' like that, and then you see the dog. The dog is stopped in its tracks, with this wonderful, white/black eye. It's stopped in its tracks—they say children and animals sense danger, they sense what's frightening. The question is: What's frightening the little boy and the dog? You look around, and you say, 'I don't know,' until you look into the wheel in the car. Oh, I say—and this is also an audience-participation painting if anyone wants to chime in. It's good that we're all standing here, because in the hubcap of the car is a mummy, and the question is where that mummy is coming from—and it's coming from kind of where we're standing. And so, the idea of the painting is that the thing to be frightened of is human beings, and this is kind of a metaphor of a human being as a mummy, and then, when you look again, you see all kinds of things that you never saw before. For instance, the woman has one arm. The woman's neck, what looks like folds of her neck could easily be gouge marks. The folds of the man's pants could be the shadow of a clawed

hand. And when you look to the left of the cigar, the last two fingers of his hand have transformed into a rat with a pink nose and a tail curled around. Everything becomes monstrous in this painting, and of course, Jim likes the collapsing of sexuality and violence, and so here's the woman's skirt hiked up above her panties, exposing her genitals—that's a common thing in Jim's work. But, if you take a look at the whole way this thing is made—the mountain, for instance—it's like he's saying he knows about twentieth-century painting. The whole middle section of that mountain is utterly abstract, but it gives the illusion of what you see in mountains, with rock formations in them, but utterly abstract. And then, if you take a look at the branch of the birch tree, or the aspen, it connects with the snow cap on the mountain, and just to show that he's a modern painter, you see some paint drips there, and then you see how he puts this dark blue thing in the sky, and if you think, 'Have I ever seen a dark blue thing like that in the sky?' and you say, 'No, I don't think I've ever seen anything like that,' so the sky is kind of grotesque. Anyway, so that blue thing, pictorially, hooks up with that white thing on the top of the mountain, and it's as though the whole painting is suspended from those two objects, anchoring things, high up on the painting. Then you see the flowers down there, looking menacing. They're too large, popping out of the bottom of the painting. And then a very clever thing he's done with the cellophane wrapping of the bread, with these little marks. And then, the 'hamburger is done' where he's just taken all the paint on his palate and mushed it together, and smeared it onto the surface. That's a very cool painting. We got it, I think, in 1974, and it's really stood up. An amazing painting really, so psychologically narratively expressionistic."

from "The Lodge" by Paul Gold

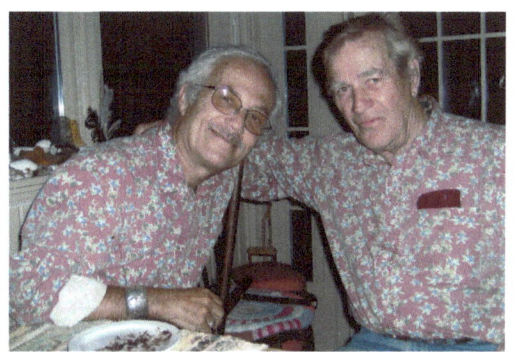

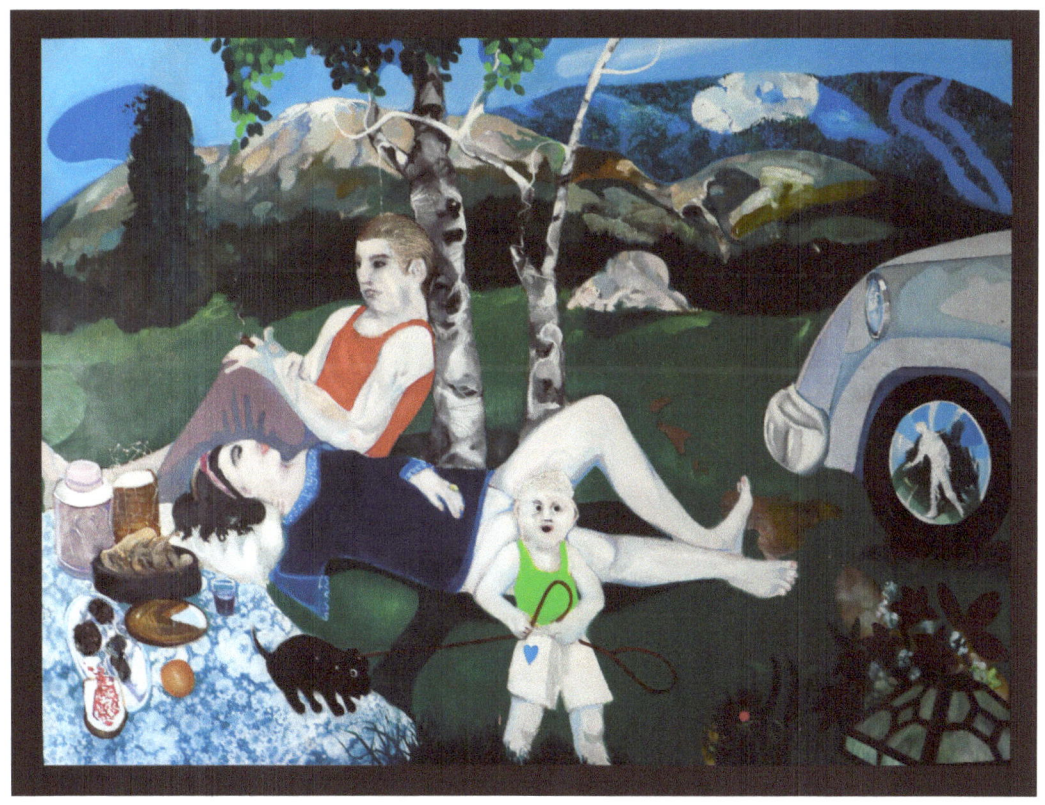

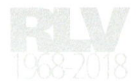

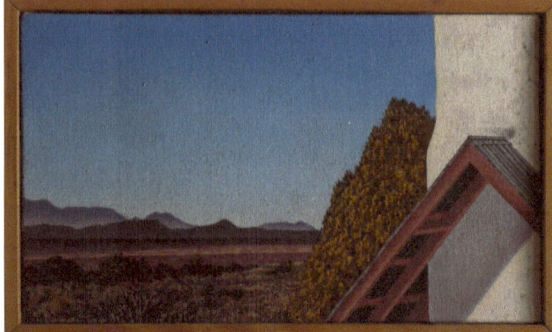

The Alterfers

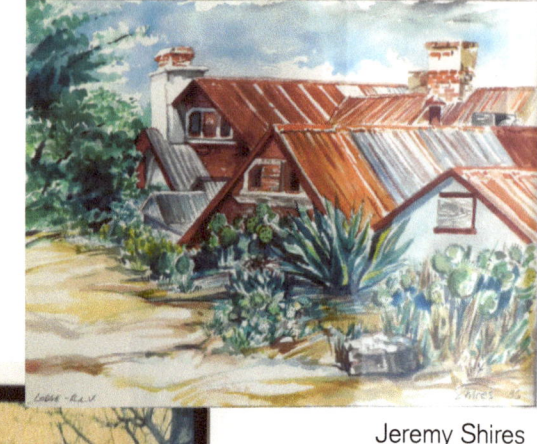

Jeremy Shires

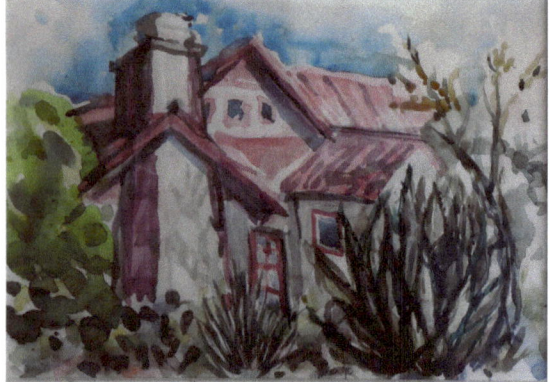

Margo Burwell

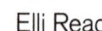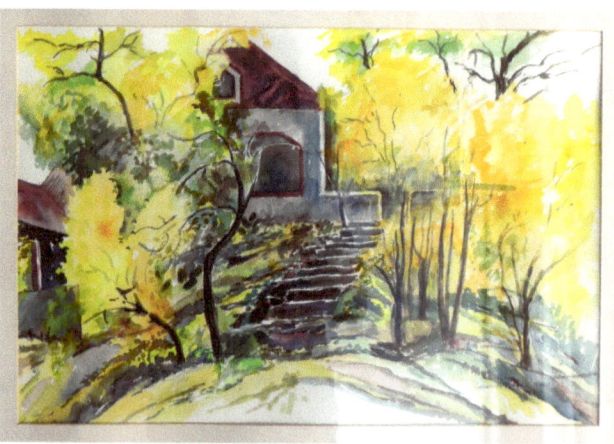

Elli Read

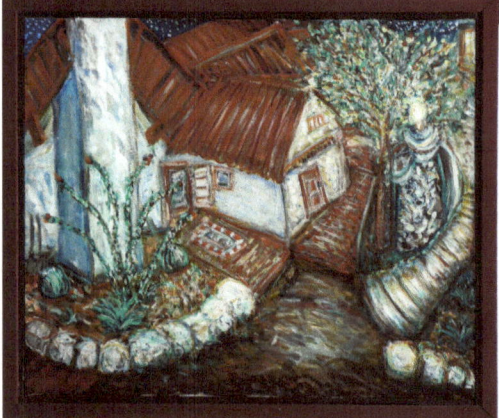

Chip Pique

The Lodge as depicted in its collection

Catherine Ferguson

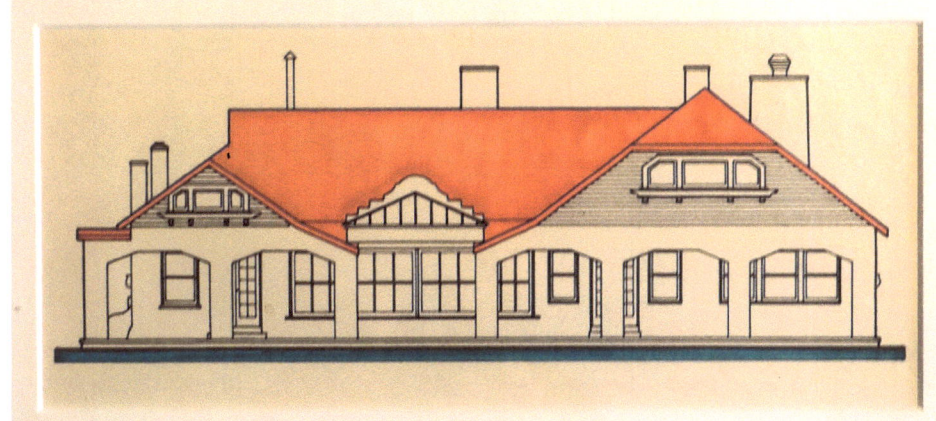

Chuck Sternberg

music and art, 2018: Austin, Wally, Andy

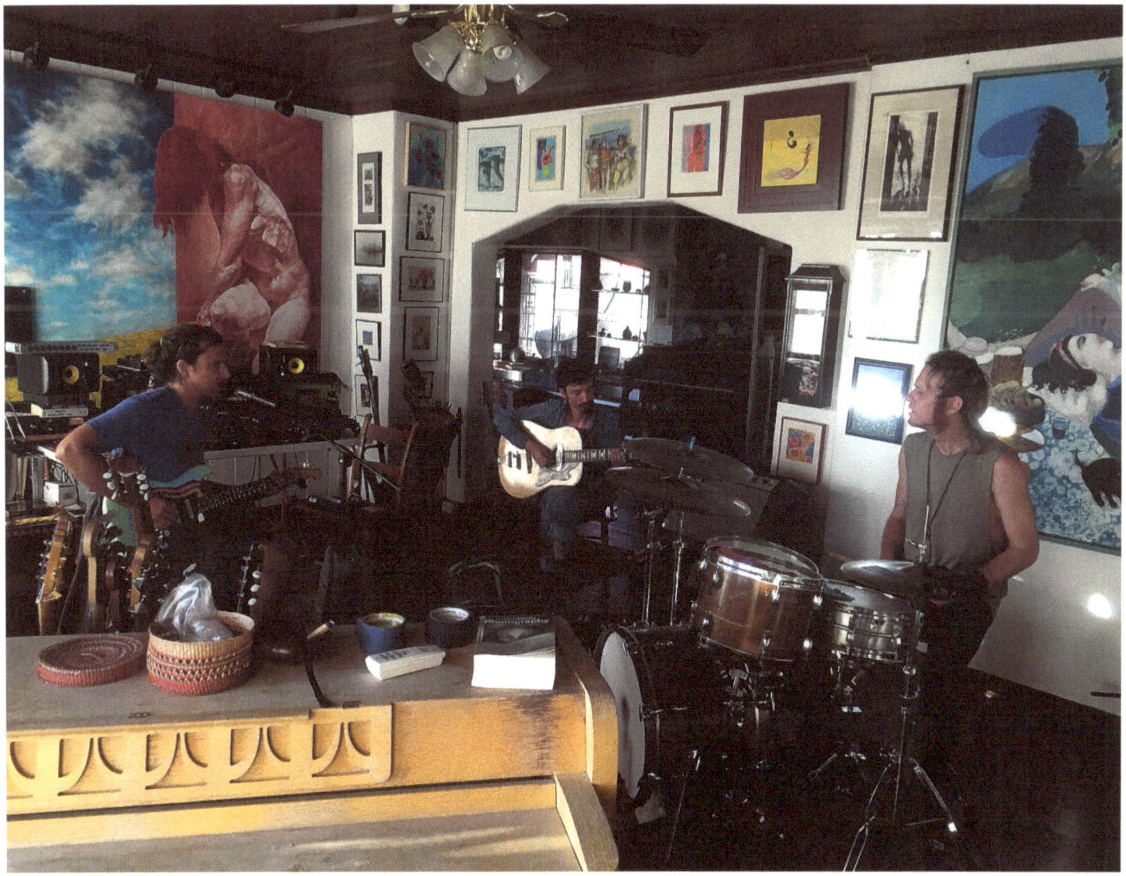

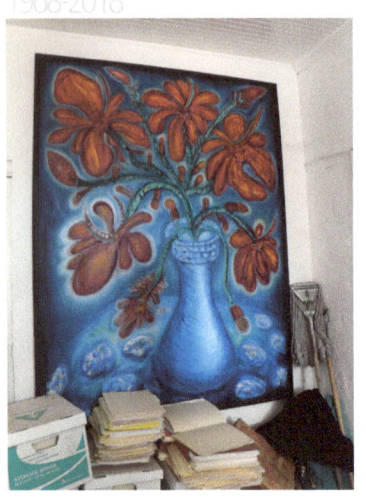

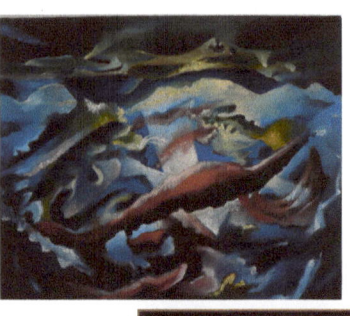

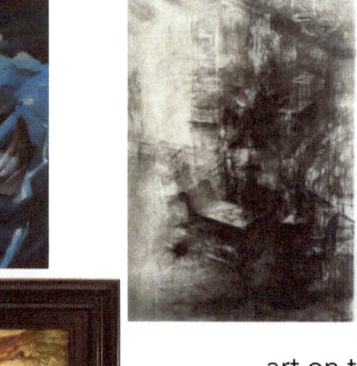

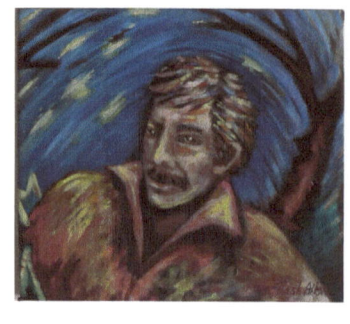

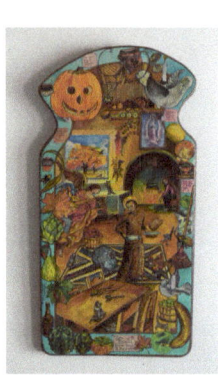

art on these pages all comes from the Nelson Collection at The Lodge. works were created by:

Chip Pique, Jim Cook, Matthias Düwel, Marie Harding, Turner Davis, Fred Haberlein, Robert Schaumbach, McWheat, Pat Dolan, Catherine Ferguson, Betsy Barnds, Steve Littler, Charles Littler, Pam Nelson, Clive Pates, Jim Davis, Paul Brach, Margo Burwell, Bernie Fierro, Saul Lieberman, George Harkins, Peggy Doogan, Andrew Rush, among the very many represented in that collection.

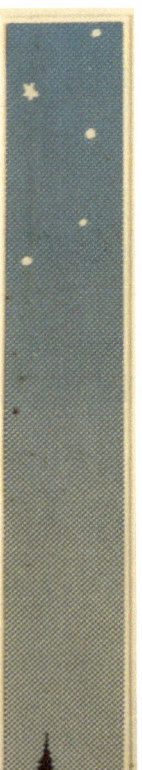

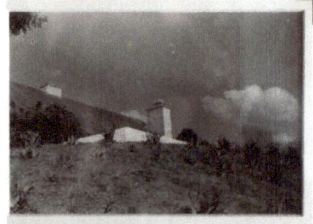

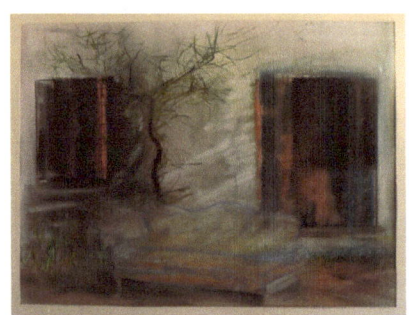

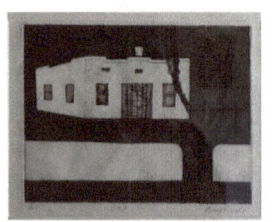

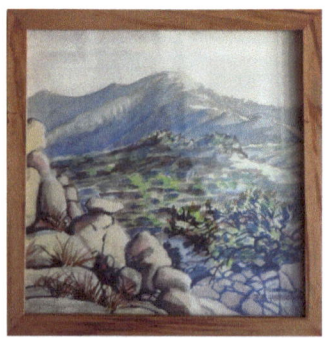

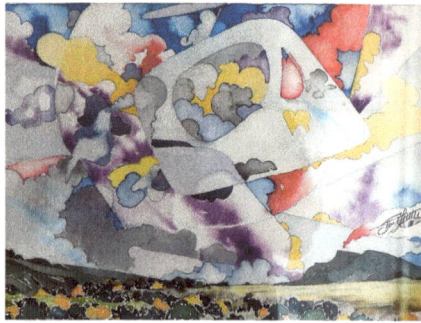

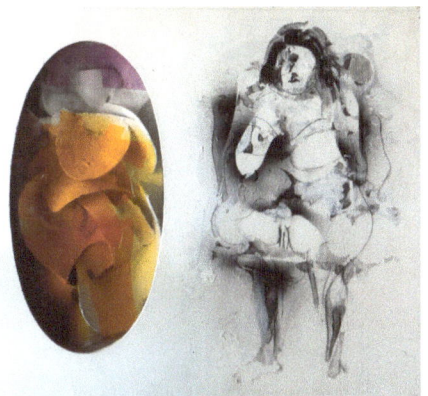
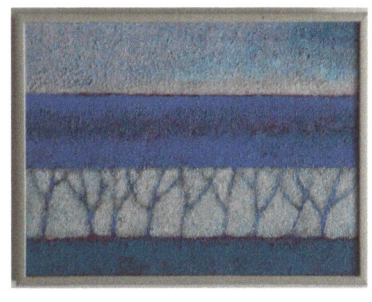
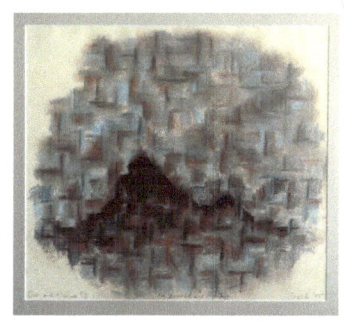

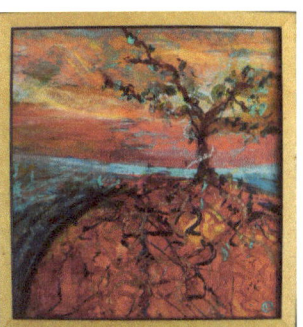
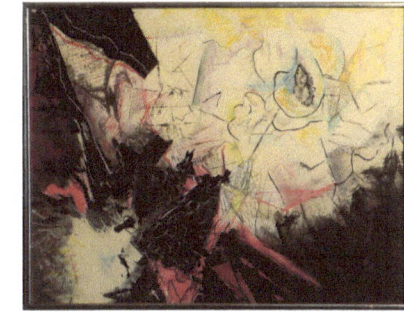
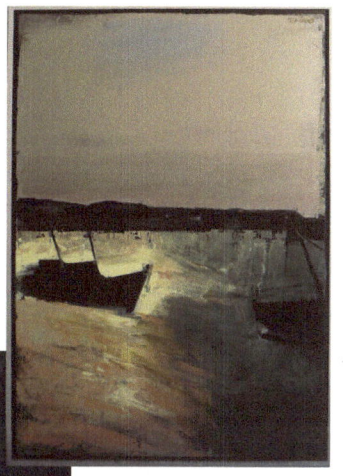

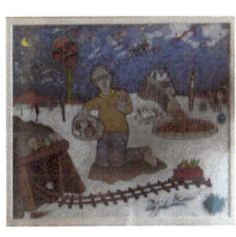
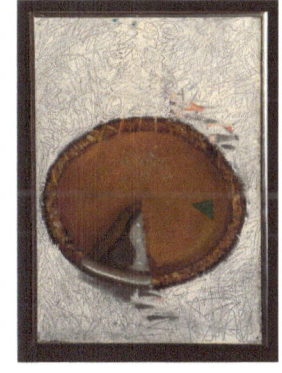
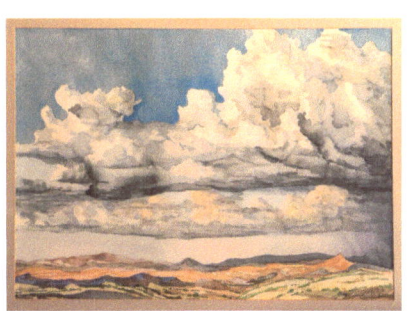

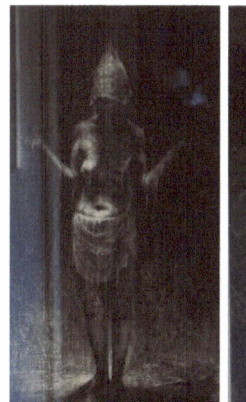
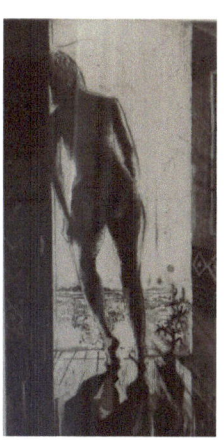

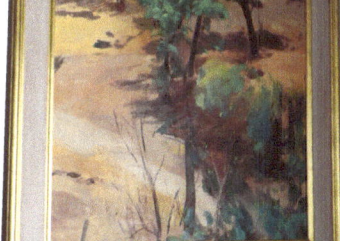

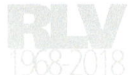

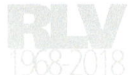

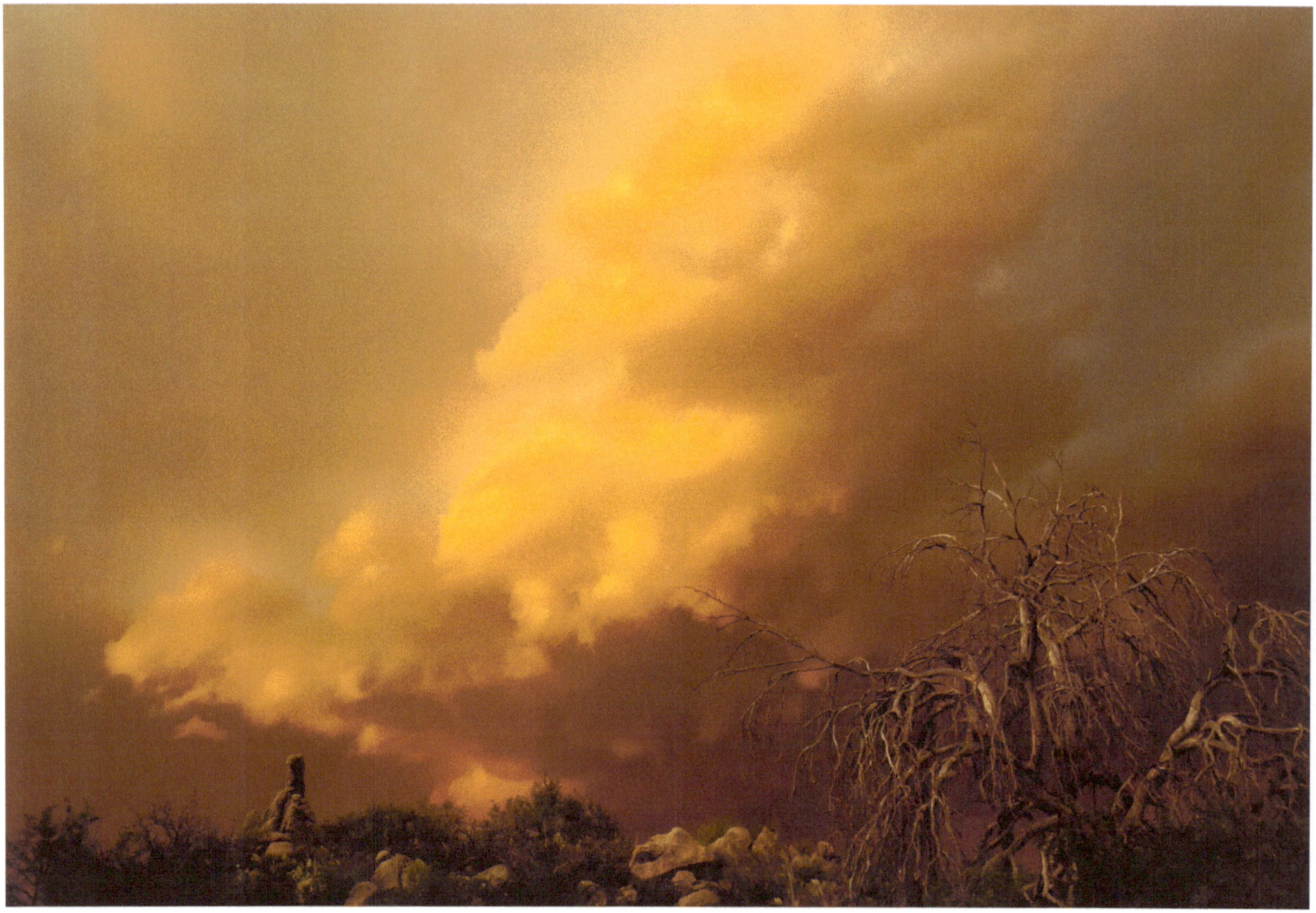

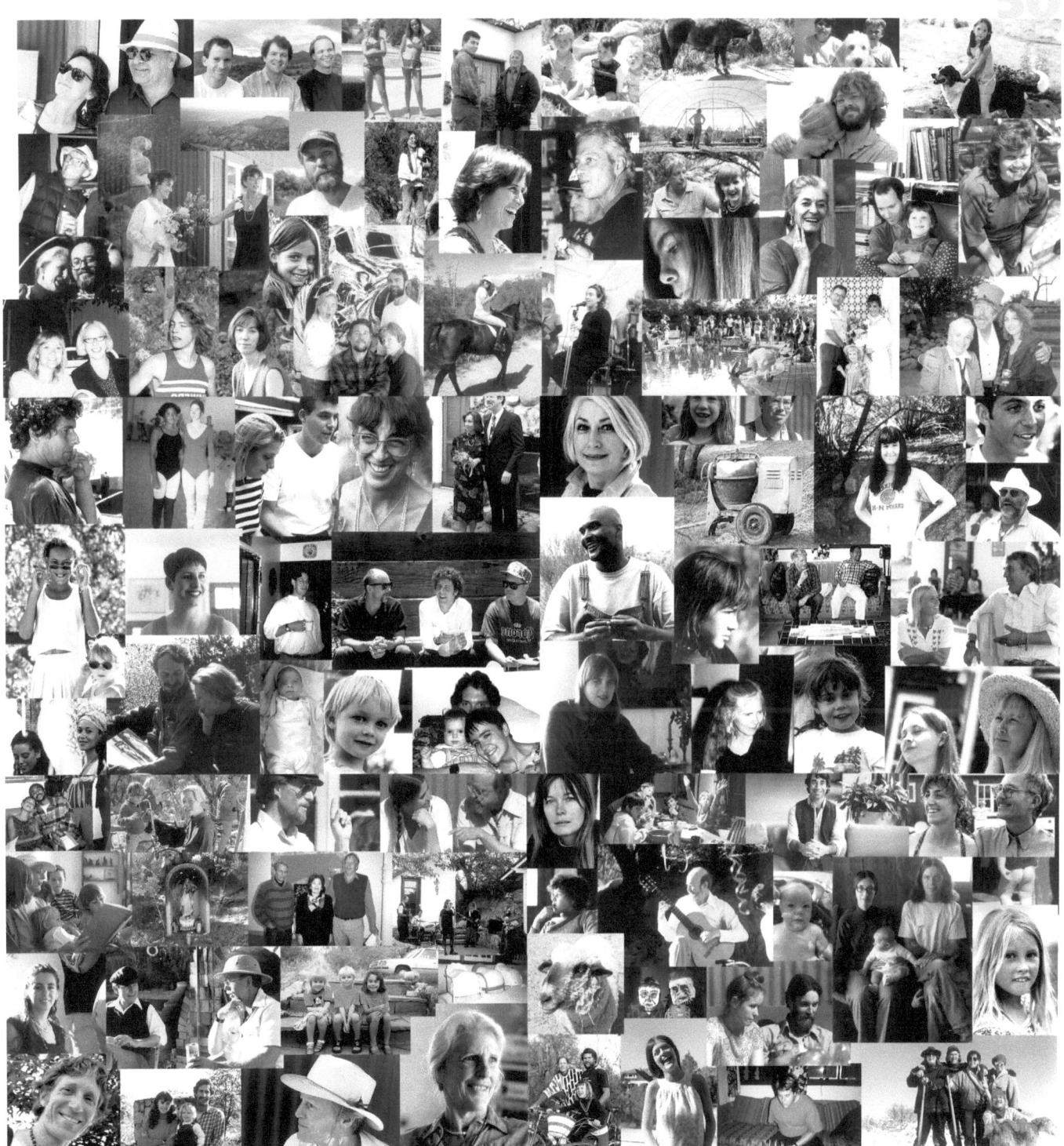

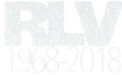

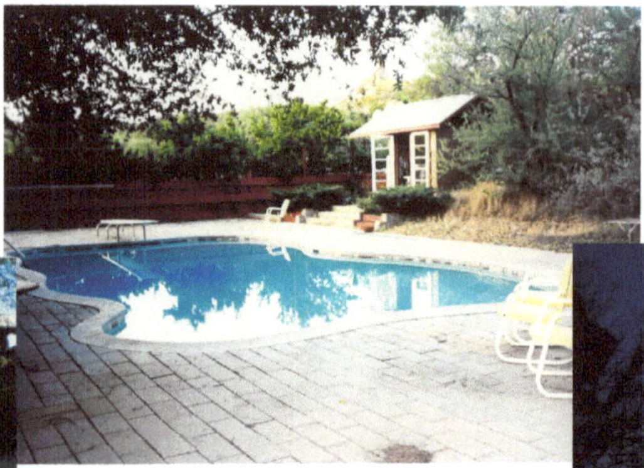

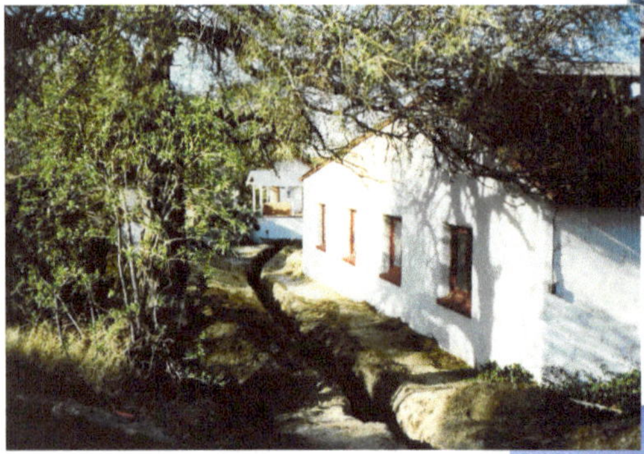

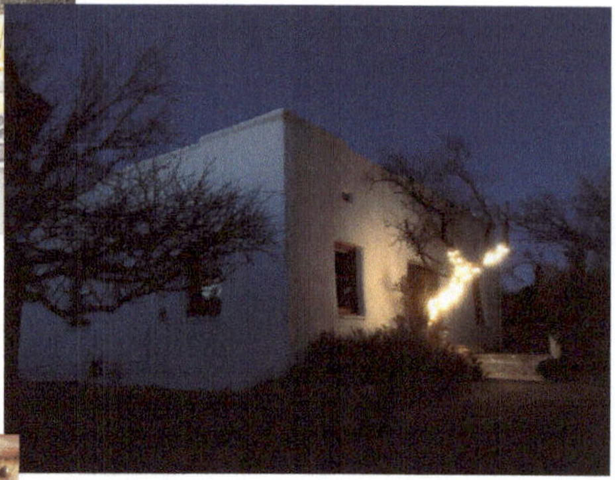

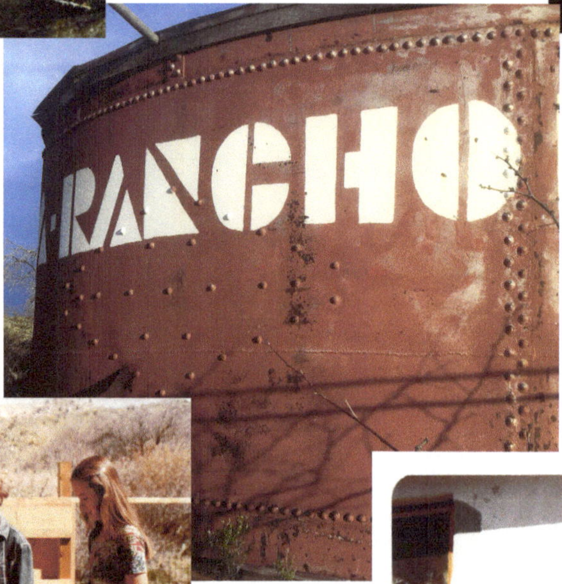

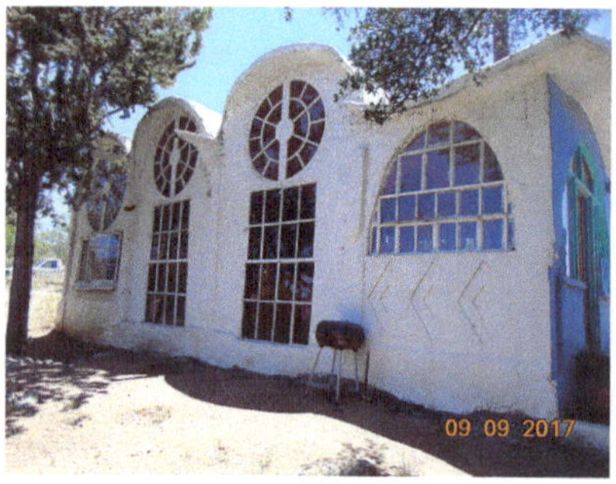

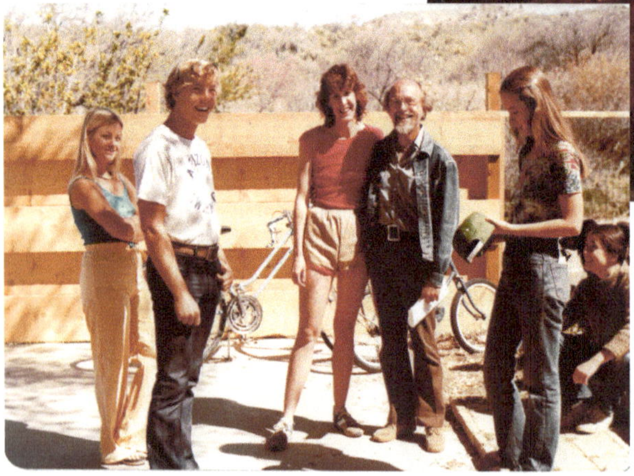

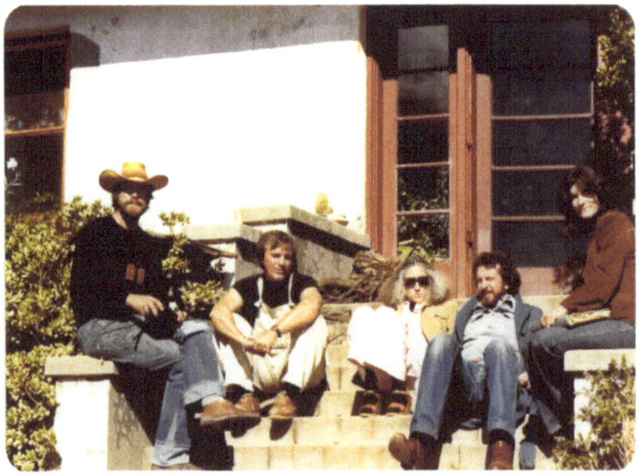

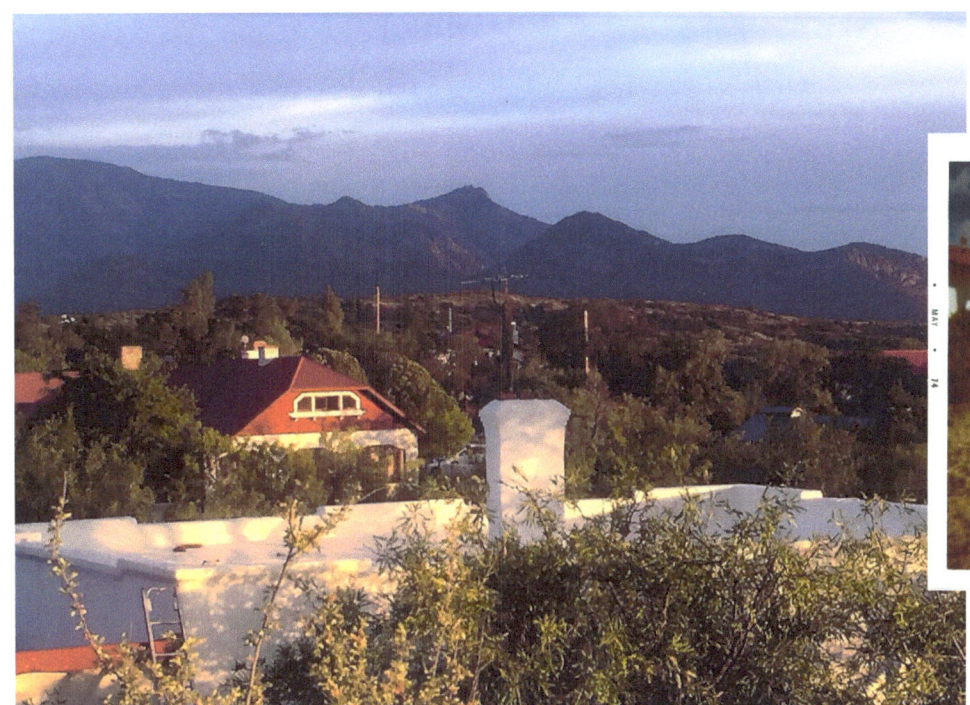

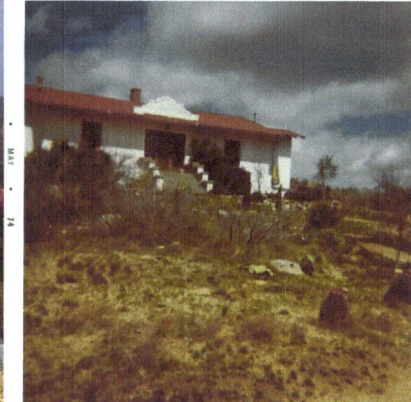

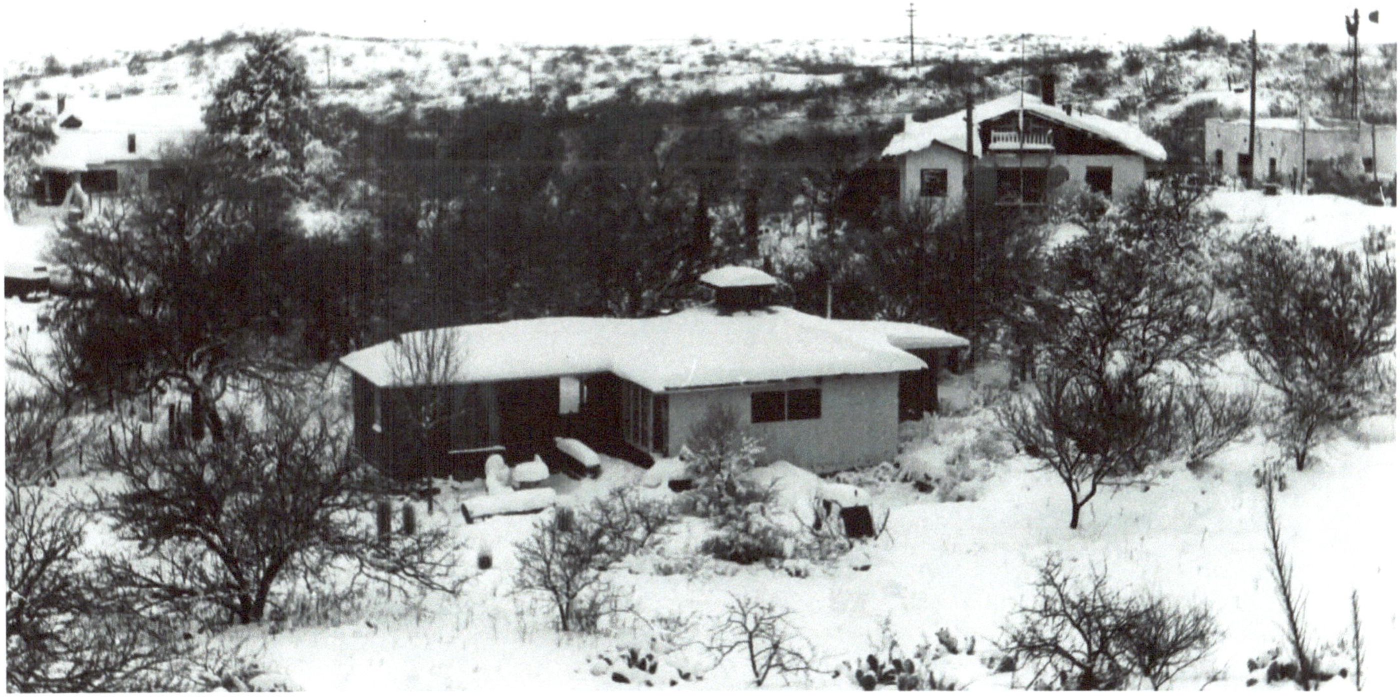

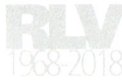

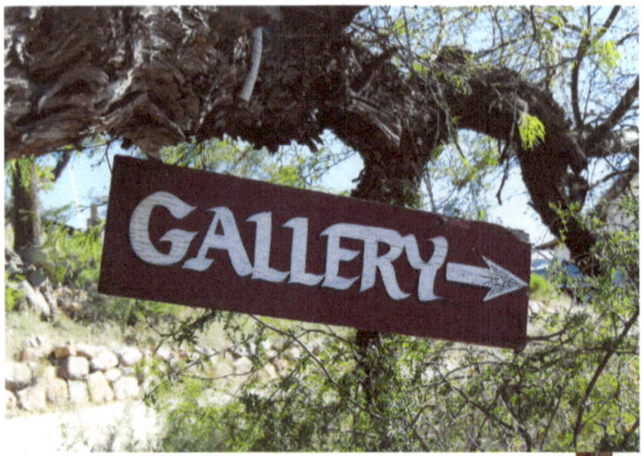

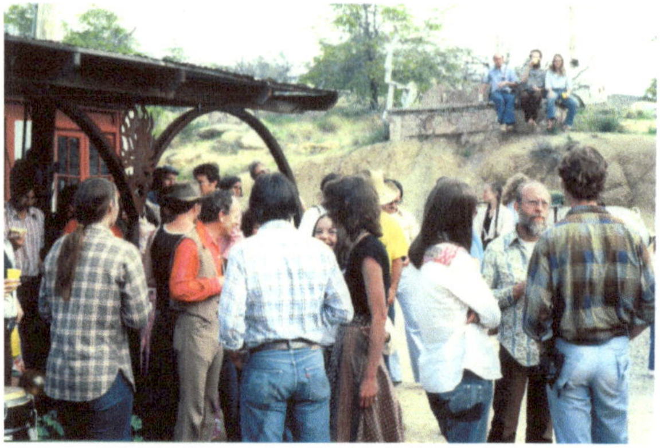

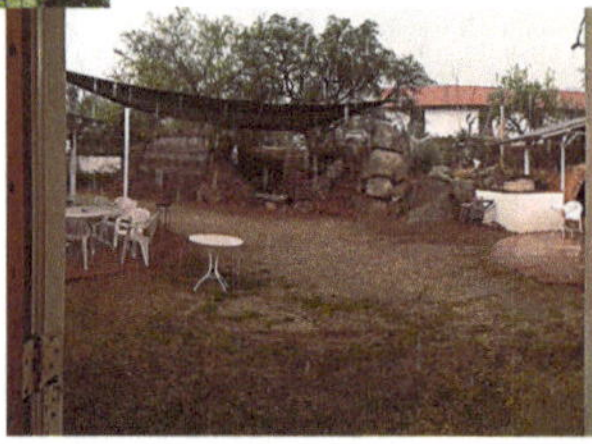

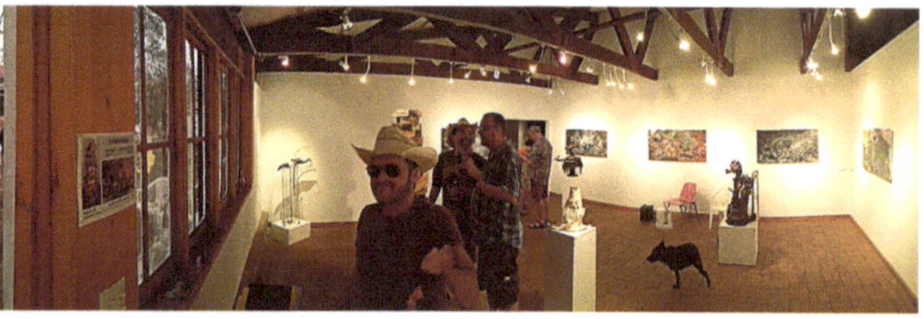

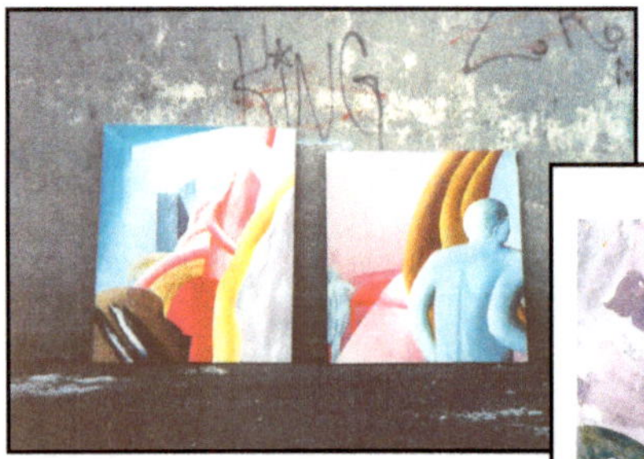

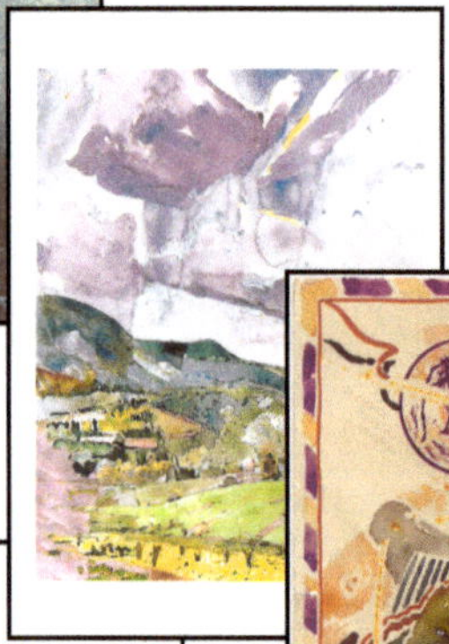

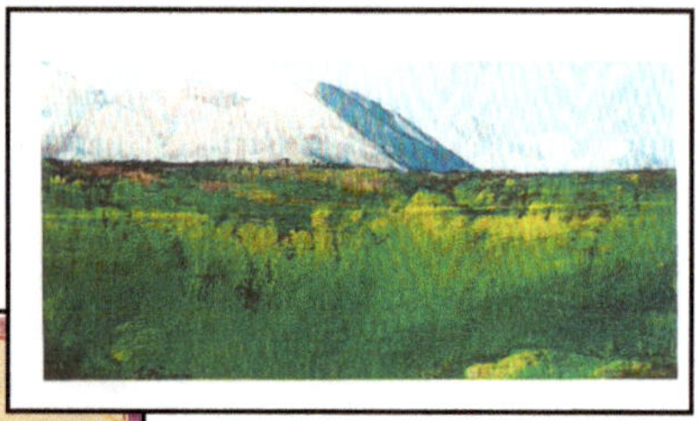

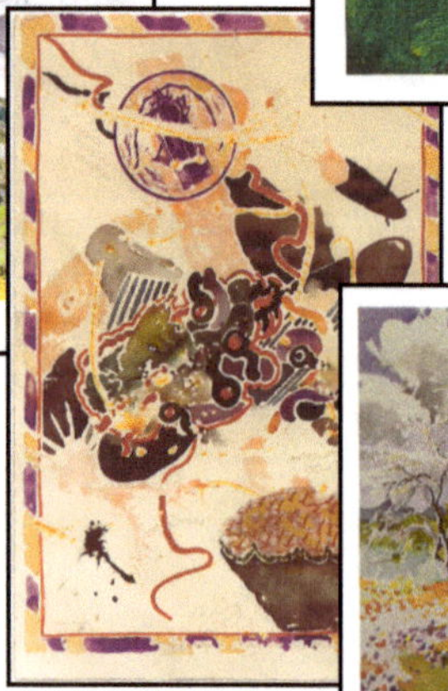

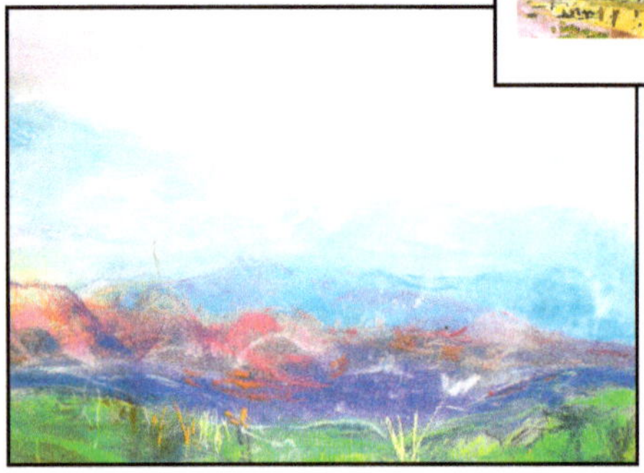

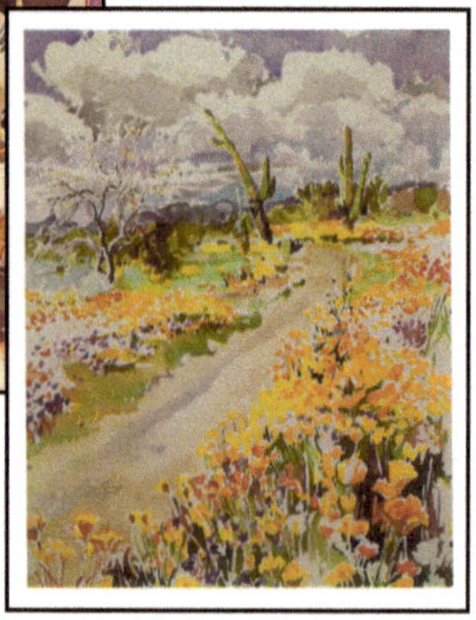

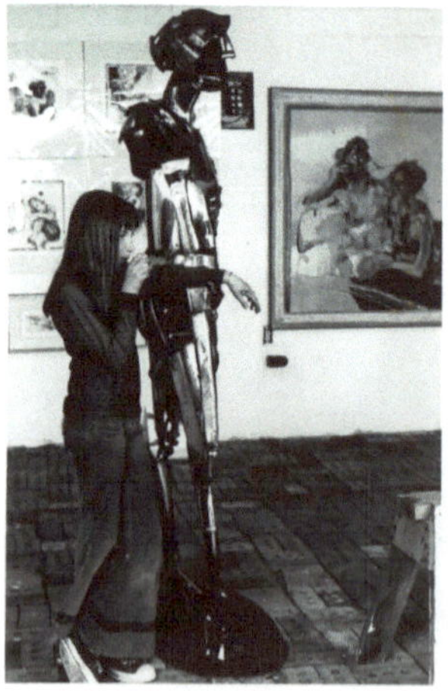

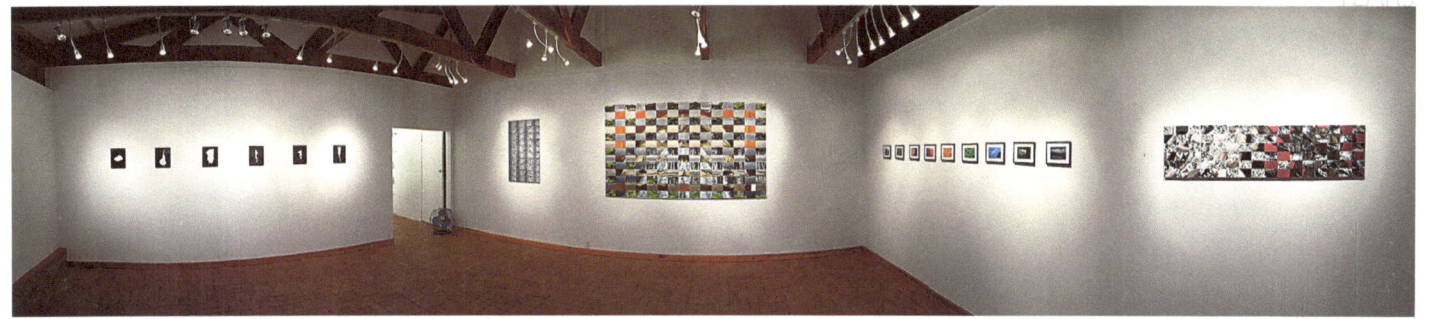

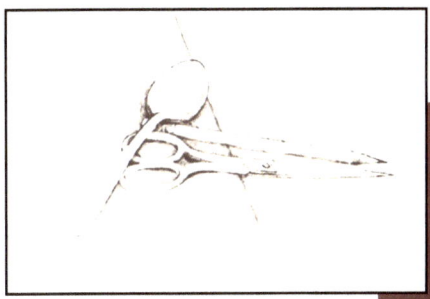

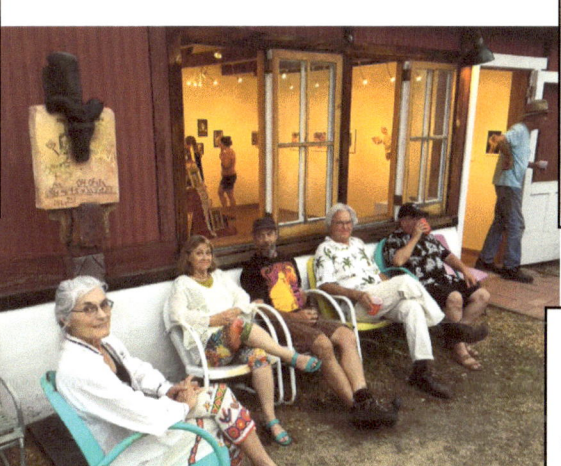

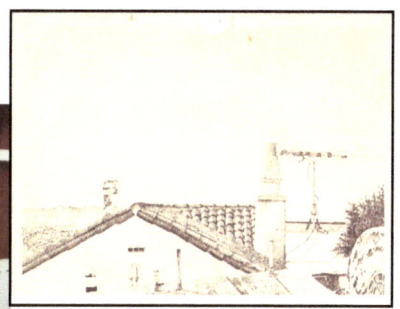

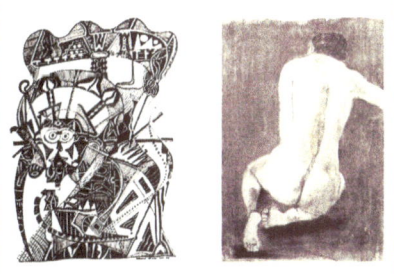

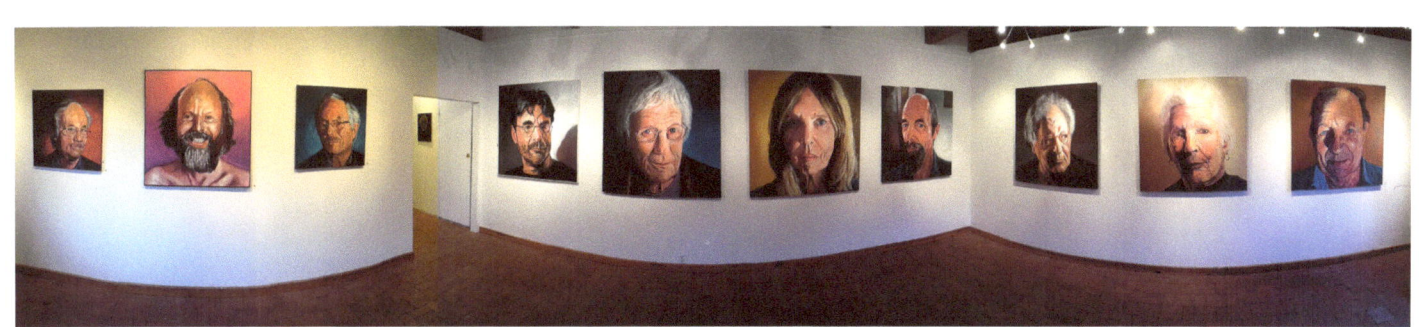

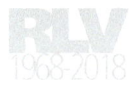

When Nobody Wore Clothes

we perch on a bookcase, arranged by age
youngest to oldest, left to right
my little sisters and I

our teenaged bodies nearly identical
same long straight blonde hair
expressions serious and wary
naked as three fawns ready to flee
captured forever in black and white

Arizona sun casts geranium
shadows on Suzanne's shoulders
Gail's bikini lines glow in summer light
she hasn't been here long
hasn't toughened her feet
to caliche and gravel washes
to mesquite thorns and prickly pear
hasn't learned the smell of creosote
bushes after the rain, the sounds
of rattlers and thrashers in the scrub

they've come from Kansas
to this desert artists' colony
to stay with me, to become friends
to separate from our parents
broken and divided as they were

we tend a vegetable garden
erect a chicken coop
laze by a swimming pool
fending off lecherous looks
from aging Lotharios

thick adobe walls shielded
us from family storms
we grew strong as saplings
when nobody wore clothes

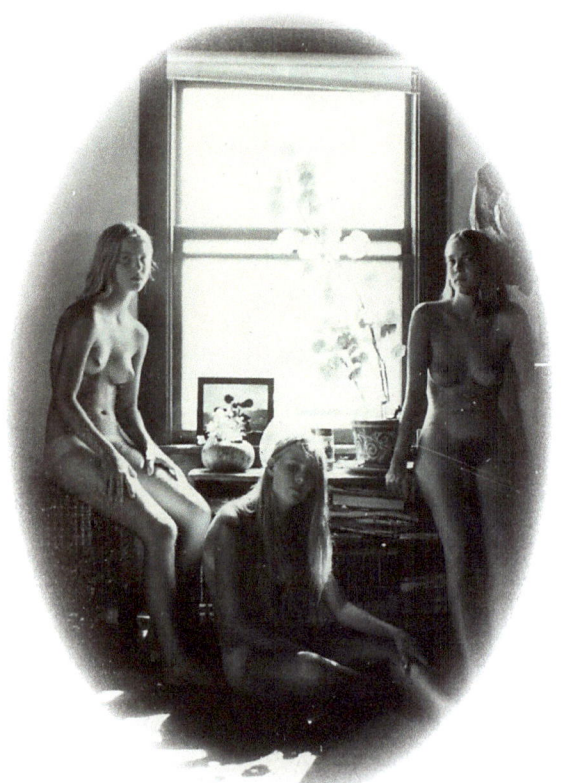

Karin Bradberry came to RLV from Prescott College in 1970 and stayed until 1973. This poem references a photo taken by Dana Slaymaker in 1972. She now lives in Los Lunas in the Central Rio Grande Valley of New Mexico.

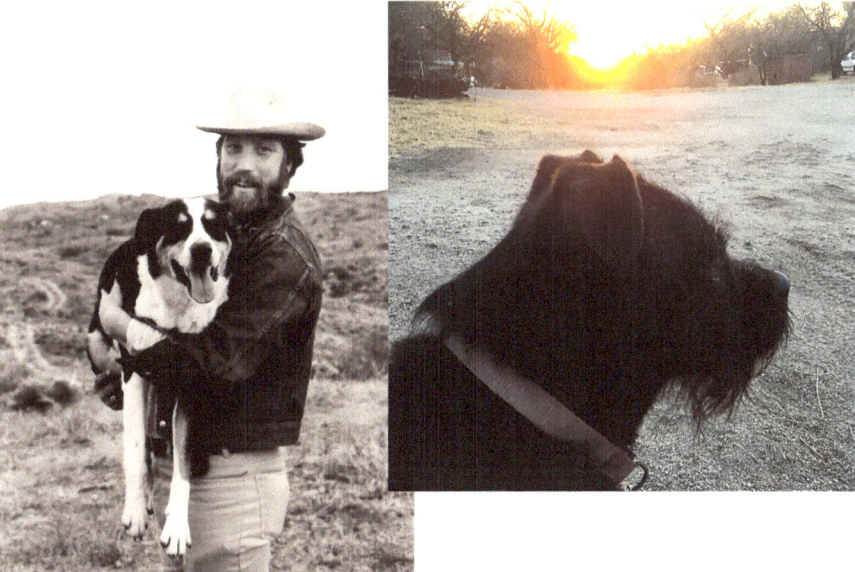

When I die,
  I want to come back
    as a Ranch dog.
    —Mary Romaniello

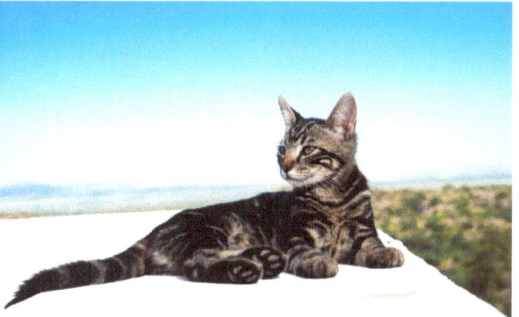

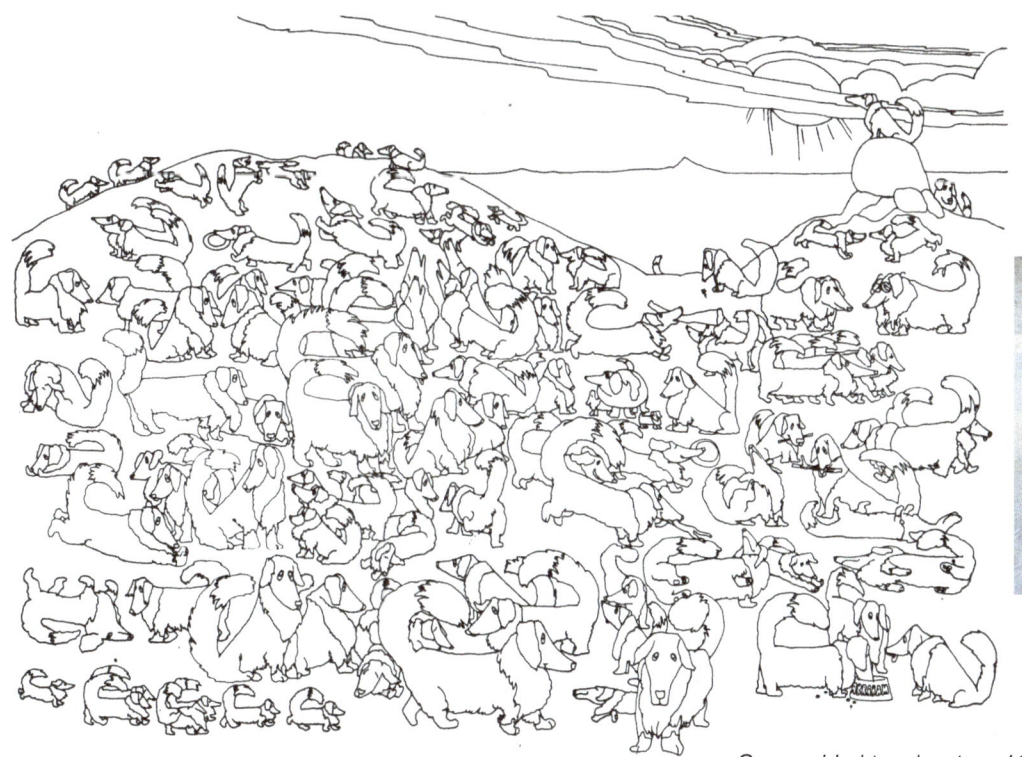

George Harkins drawing: 100 Abrahams

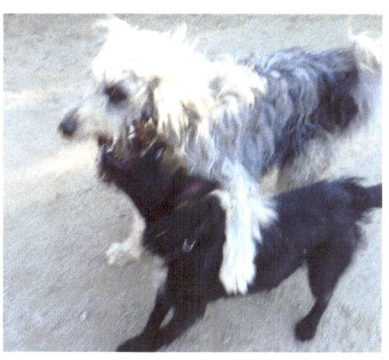

35

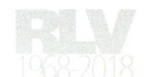

In Memoriam

CLAUDE BAILEY

GREG BENDER

ROY BONGARTZ

PAUL BRACH

TONY CHERRY

JAMES G. DAVIS

ELLIE DOOGAN

KATHRYN FERGUSON

CHIRINE AL-KHADEM

FRED HABERLEIN

DRUMMOND HADLEY

ALAN HARRINGTON

EUGENE "SKIP" HARWICK

JOHN HUGGLER

MARDEAN HUGGLER

CHARLES LITTLER

SAM BUTTERY LITTLER

ELIZABETH MANFREDI

BRUCE MCGREW

MINNIE NELSON

DON NORMARK

JOANNA PELED

EDWARD PUTZAR

YAEKO PUTZAR

MARCIA SCHEER

ARTIS SCHROEDER

MIRIAM SCHAPIRO

SUZANNE SMITH

JOCK SNEDDEN

JOI STEPHENS

LARRY STURHAHN

CK WILLIAMS

ANN WOODIN

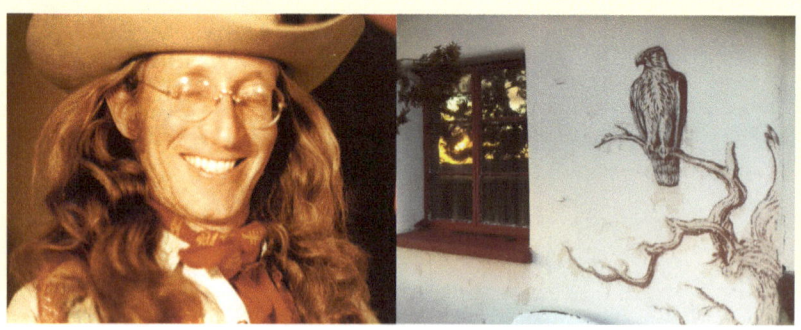

FRED HABERLEIN
1944–2018

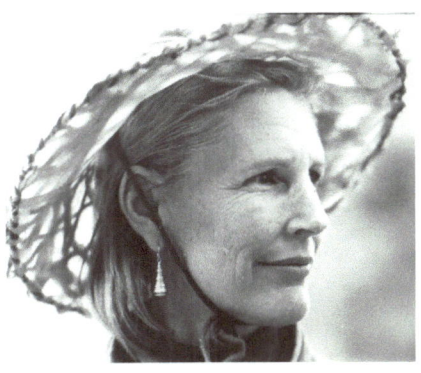

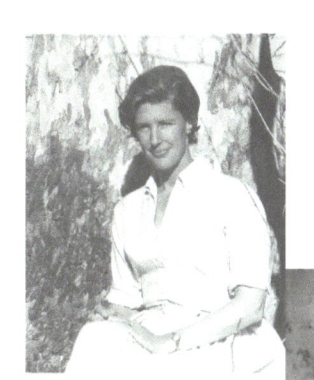

Ann Woodin
1926–2017

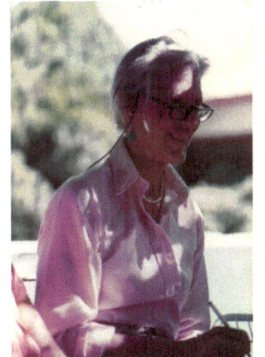

You don't have to agree in order to reach consensus as long as, when push comes to shove, you have your shoulders to the same wheel—the well-being of our community. I learned this at the meeting where I realized that the nincompoop spouting nonsense on the other side of the room cared for this place as much as I did.

— from the Postscripts in the
'Customs & Agreements'
booklet Ann wrote

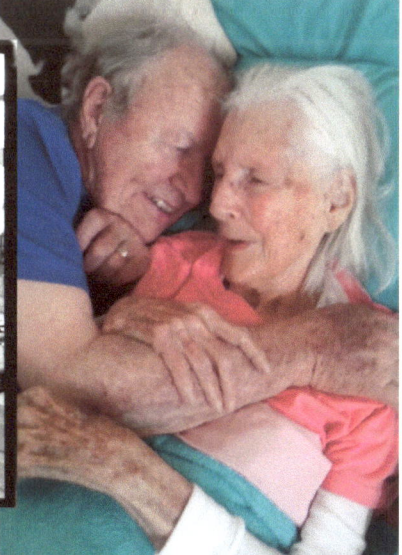

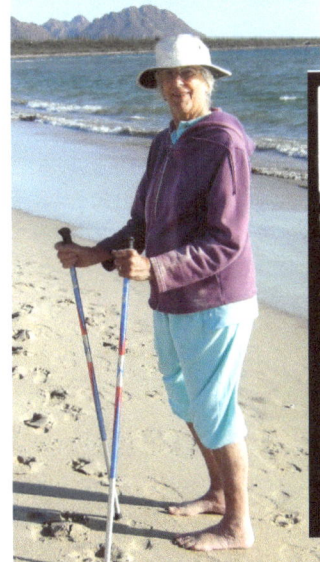

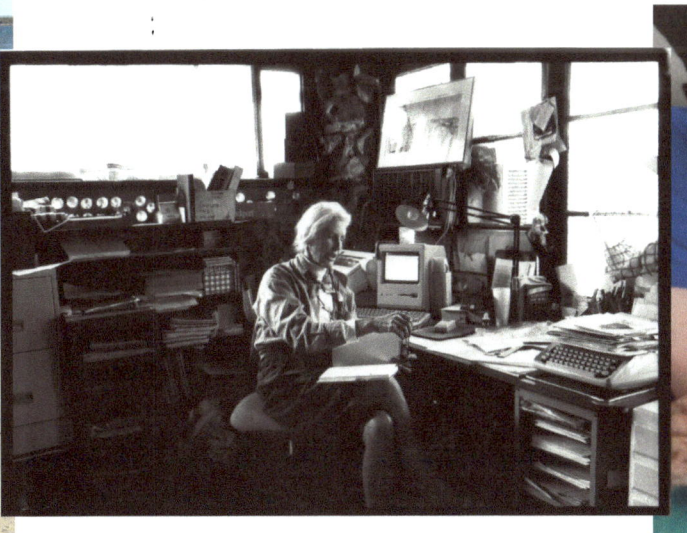

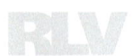

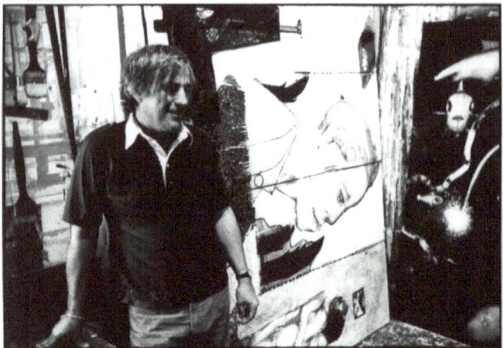

JAMES G. DAVIS
1931—2016

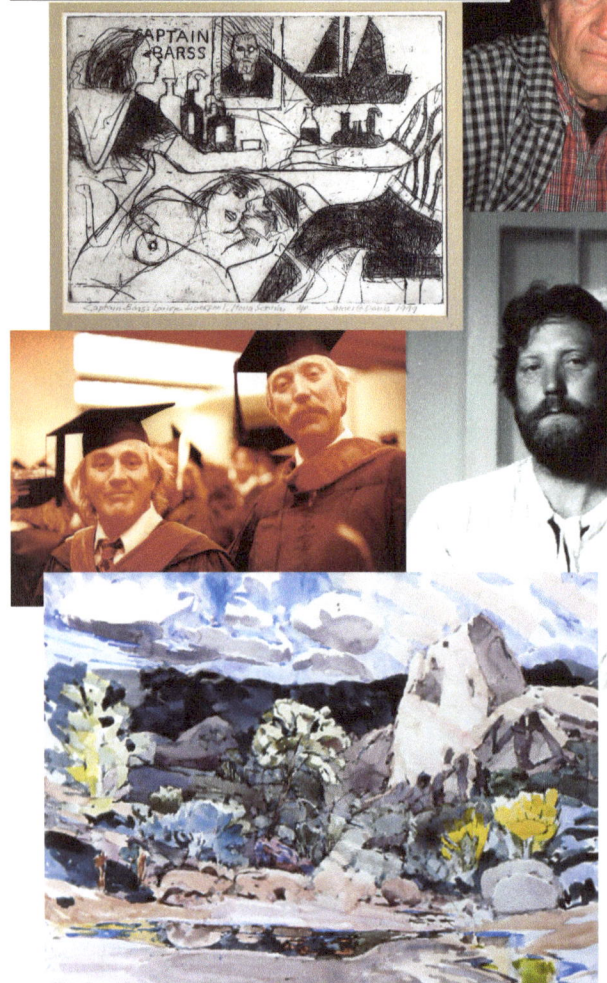

BRUCE MCGREW
1937—1999

CHARLES LITTLER
1928–1991

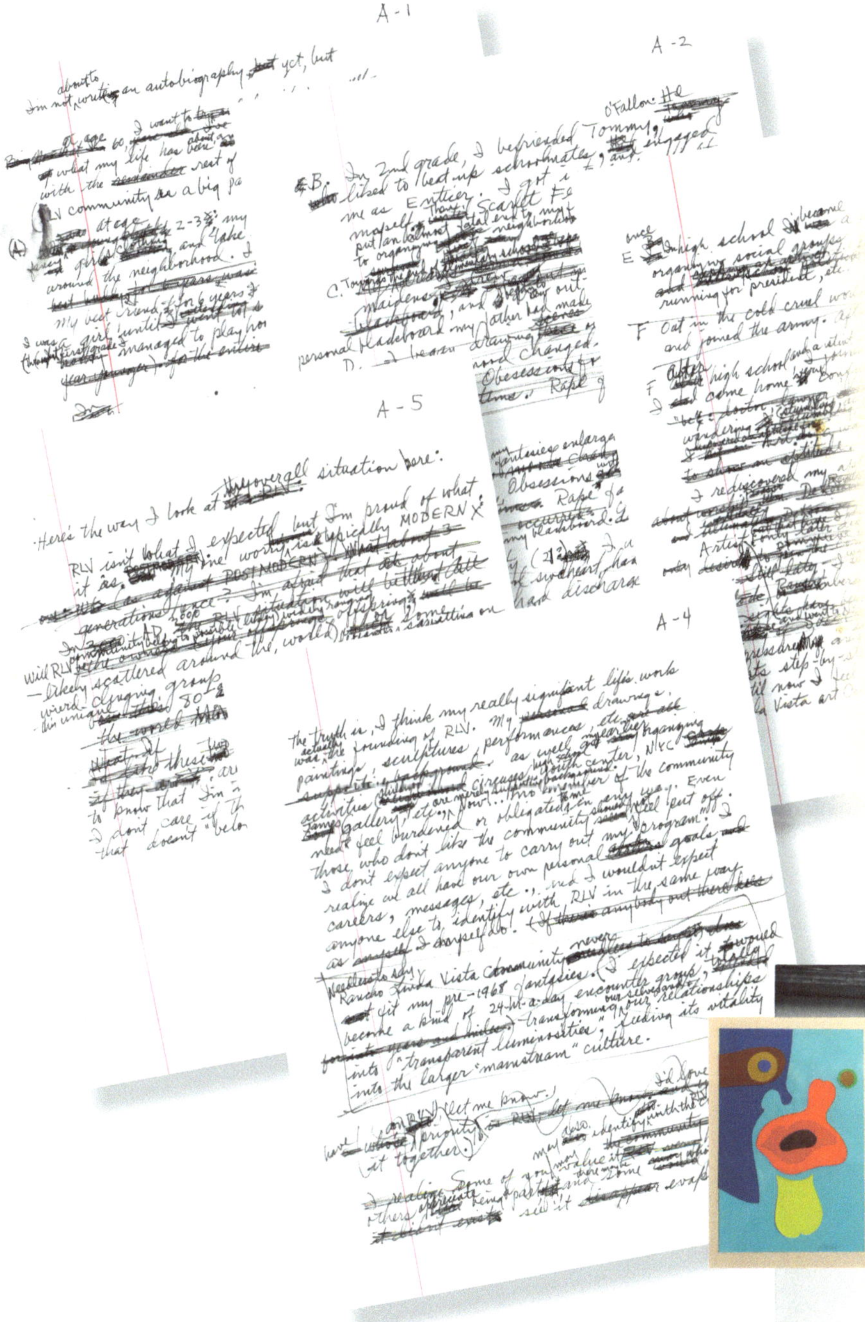

Needless to say, Rancho Linda Vista community never fit my pre-1968 fantasies. I expected it would become a kind of 24-hr-a-day encounter group. Totally transforming ourselves and our relationships into "transparent luminosities," feeding its vitality into the larger "mainstream" culture.

Some of you may identify with the RLV community, some may value it highly as members, others appreciate being a part, and there may be some who'd just as soon see it evaporate.

The truth is, I think my really significant life's work was actually the founding of RLV….

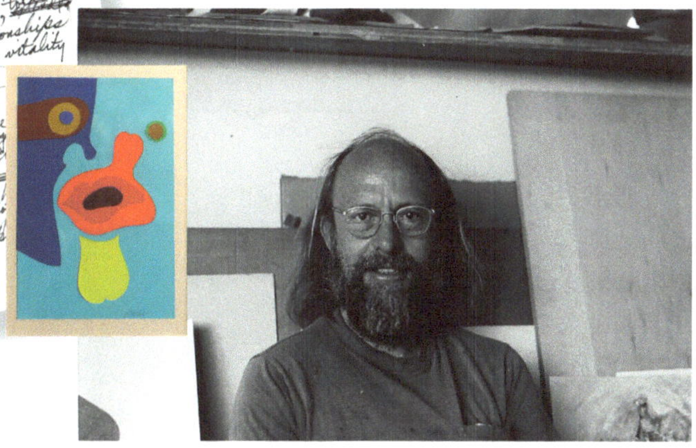

pages from one of Charles' late notebooks

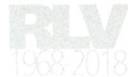

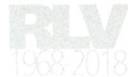

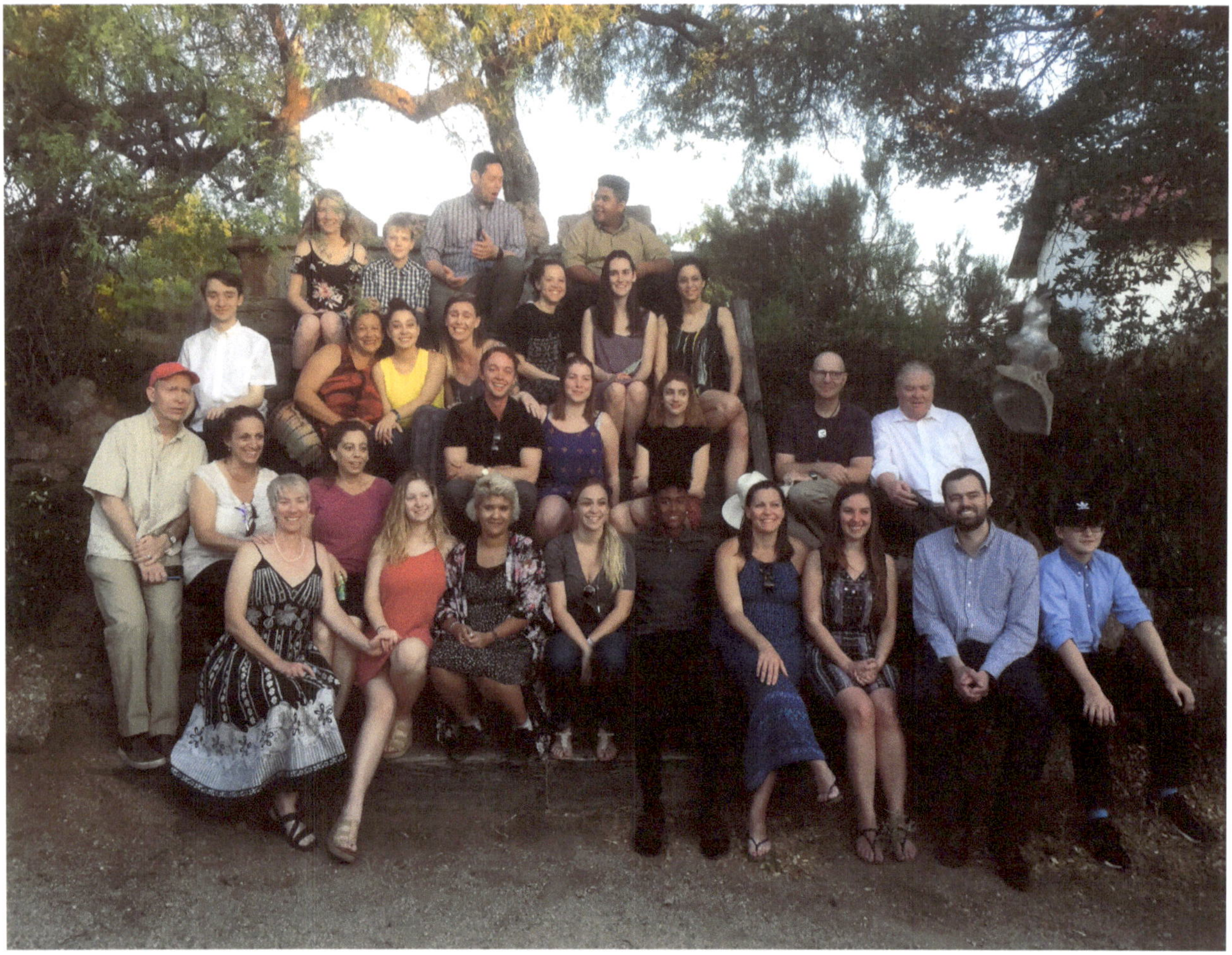

assembled group of the "3rd Generation"- kids of Ranch kids
with friends & "2nd Generation" relatives at Ann Woodin's memorial,
2017

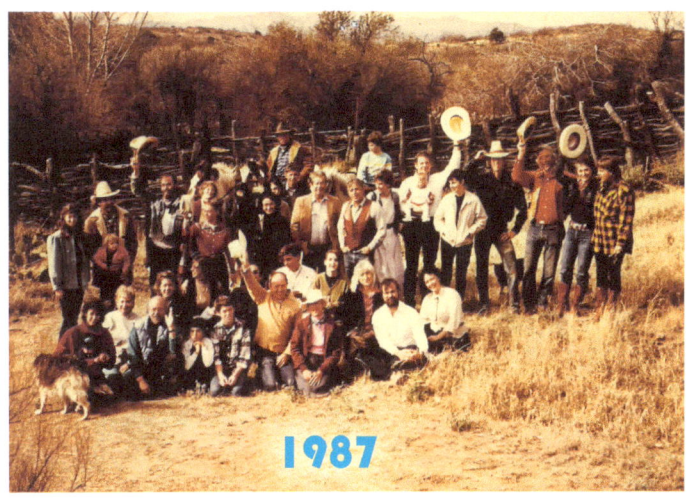

1987

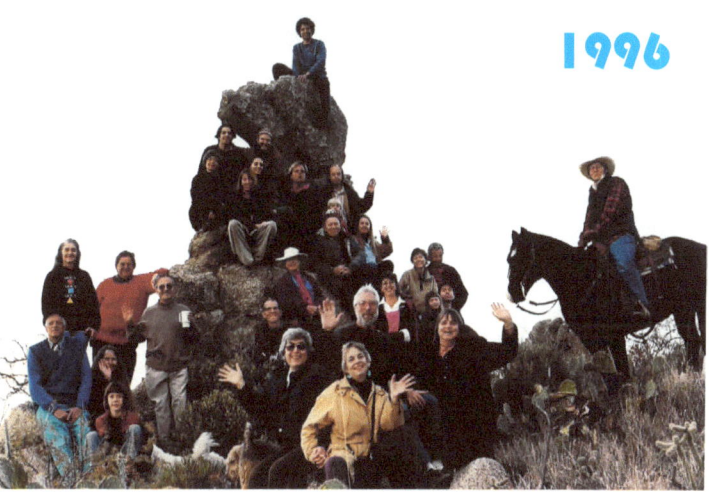

1996

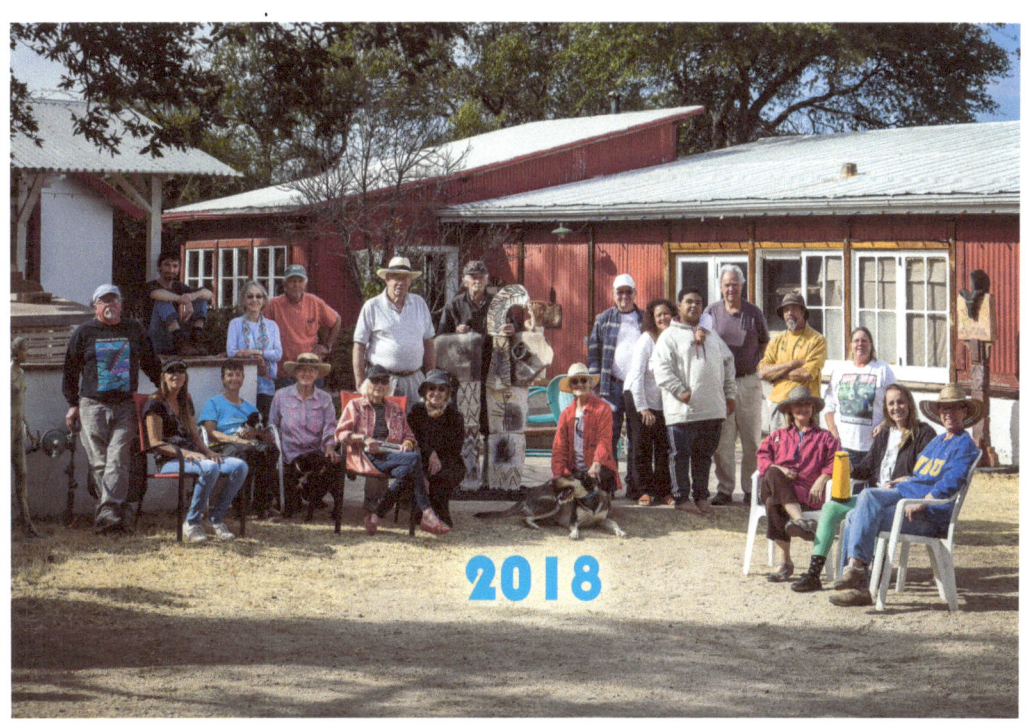

2018

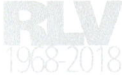

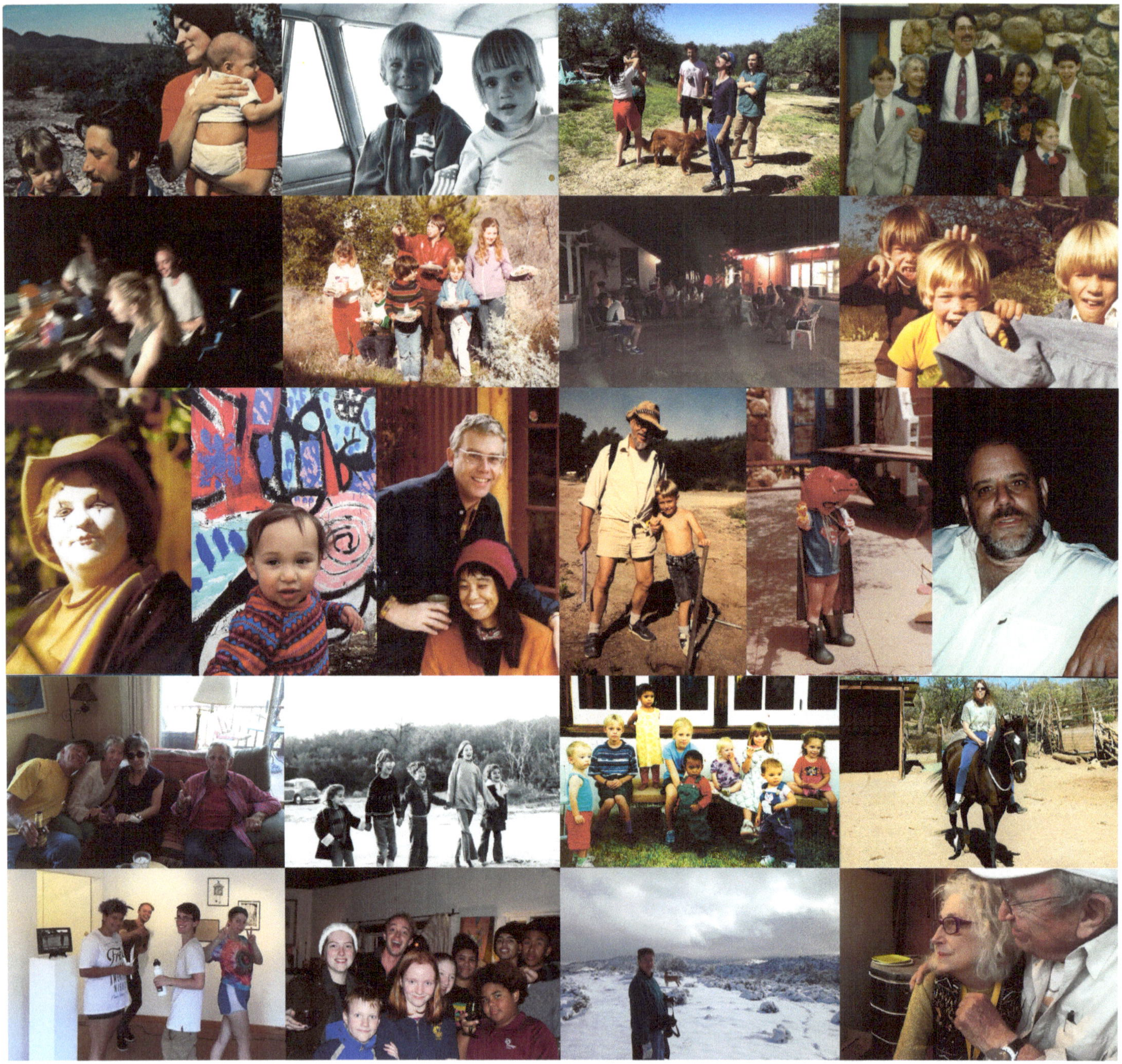

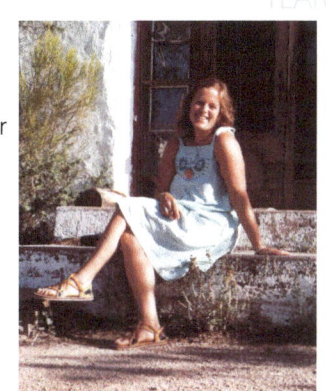

My relationship with the Ranch goes back to 1978 when I first moved to Oracle. After initially being invited to one of the Ranch events, over the years I got to know and care about those who lived, visited, and worked there. The new generation whom I haven't gotten to know as well and the children who are now married and young adults especially strike me now! They were all so talented, interesting and adorable; it has been an honor watching them grow. Maggie and Sam and I worked together sanding for Van in his shop for a time when they were in their teens. Participating in a few of the group effort baby quilt creations for the newborns over the years was always full of camaraderie. The Bathhouse was a favorite for hot tubbing and later the awesome quiet meditation in the sensory deprivation tank.

Later, while living in Bootbar, I was fortunate to read one of my early works with Bill Root and Pam Uschuk in the barn gallery one evening. It was a transformative experience. The ranch atmosphere has always fostered and supported creativity. Pat, Charles, Patrick and family felt like a home away from home and I was always amazed and participating in Pat's explorations and expressions using different media. Especially the years of Patrick's video stardom and later with shamanic journeying and drumming circles. We had a "sistahood" of sorts and I will always treasure that. Charles' enlisted me in creating my own iteration of one of his string art creations that he wanted to sell at Sears for, I think, $24.95 to encourage people to experience their own creativity. That was another transformative experience for me. Charles' influence, encouragement, friendship, and support meant the world. Bruce opened me to the experiencing abstract art and the vibration of color. There are too many gifts of connection to mention here from years of encounters with so many.

I've loved all the celebrations, holidays, exhibitions; meeting and getting to know the work and personas the ranch and of visiting artists, musicians and poets; evening games, dancing in the moonlight, parties, dinner gatherings and long walks down or above the wash. One of my early favorite events was the 4th of July boat contest where floatable boats were created for the pool with such ingenuity. There were

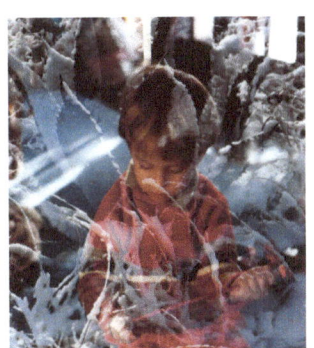

always enlightening discussions at the kitchen table with Arnold, Marilyn and others and those amazing Thanksgiving potlucks at the Lodge. But the varied and inspiring works of all the resident, visiting and exhibiting artists, writers, and musicians has enriched and informed my own artistic journey. Living in Tucson and missing much of RLV in the 21st century until recently, it's interesting to hear of the younger generation's influence in reinventing the mission of RLV and initiating greater community outreach.

—*Junardi Armstrong*

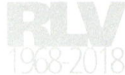

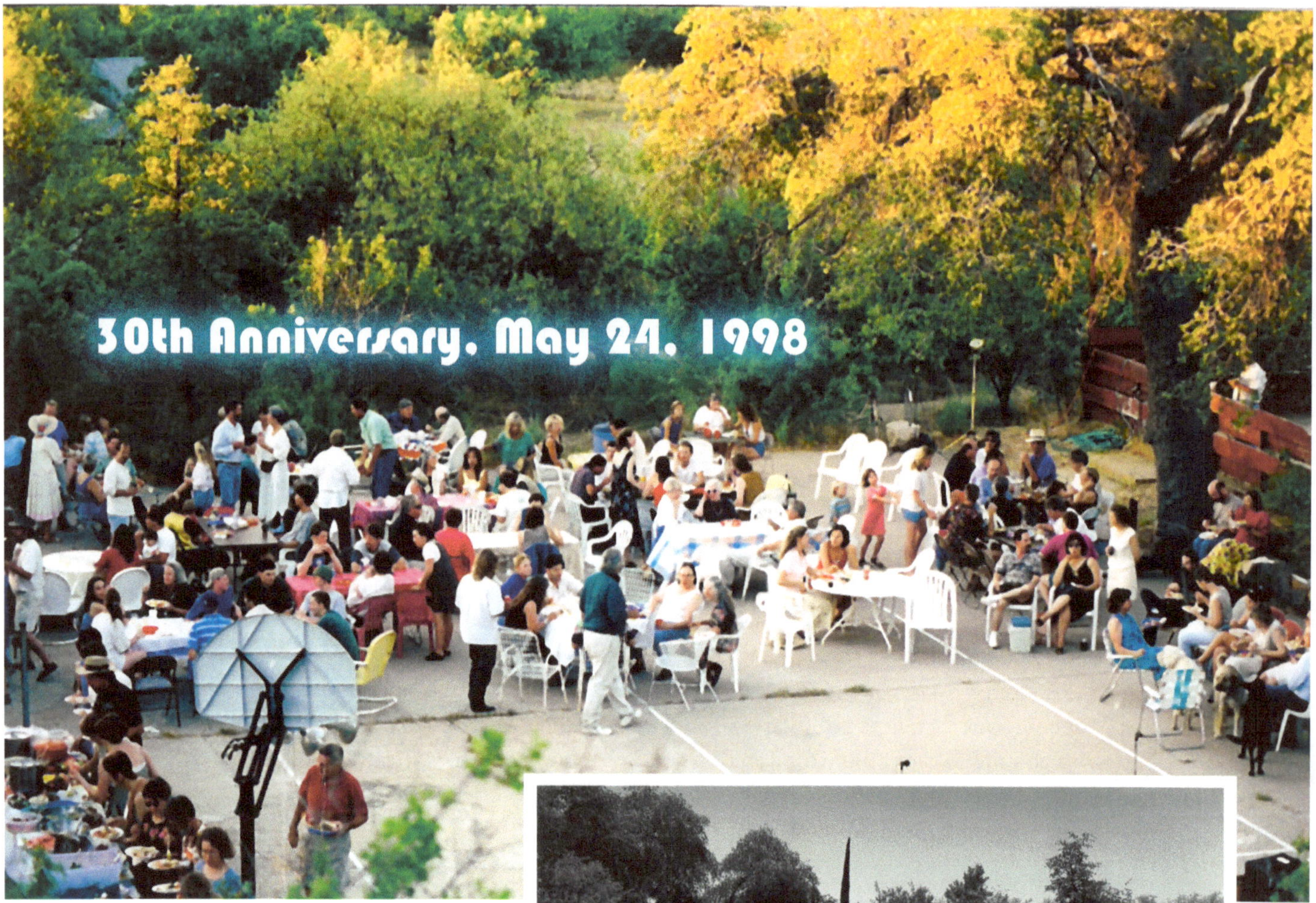

30th Anniversary, May 24, 1998

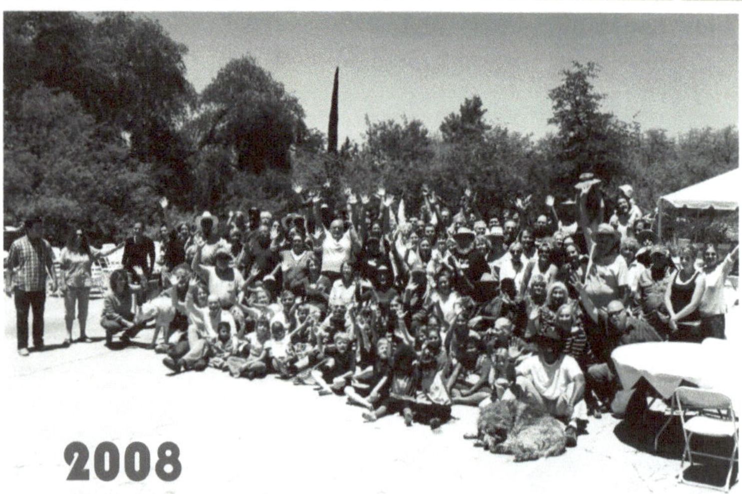

2008

*Dana Slaymaker top photo,
Edward Putzar. bottom and opposite*

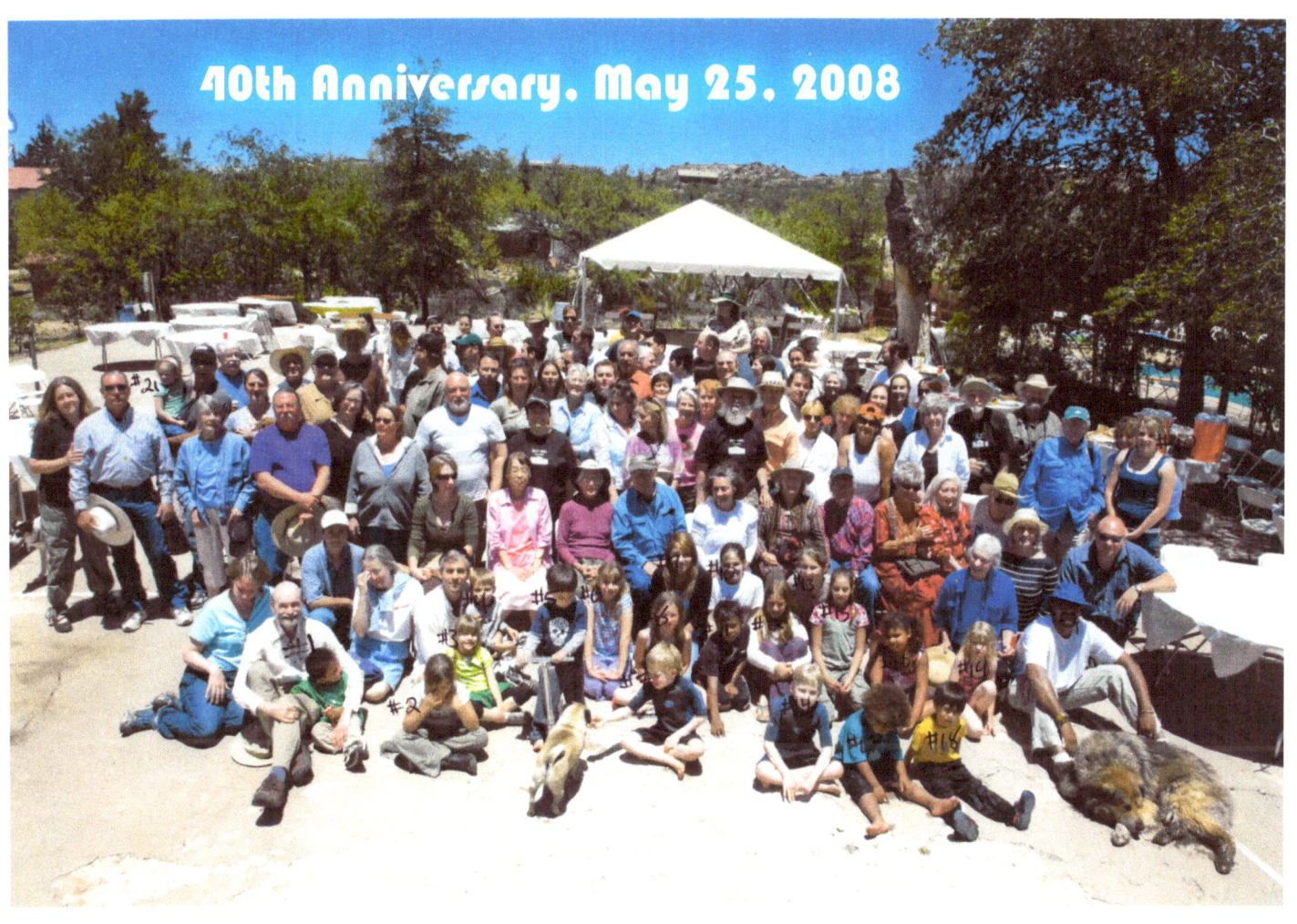

40th Anniversary, May 25, 2008

Photographs in this book were taken or provided by :

Dana Slaymaker
Edward Putzar
Ivy Simone Miller
Shelley McGrew
Maggie Miller
Stroud & Cynthia Watson

Larry Sturhahn
MaryAnne Davis
Fox McGrew
David Jaffrey
Andy Rush
Pat Dolan

Nicolas Baird
Imo Baird
Ray Manley

and many others
we were unable to identify

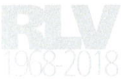

So we are now a corporation, complete with articles, by-laws, a president, secretary, treasurer and a five-person board of directors. Even so, our real organizational structure is anarchical rather than democratic. There is no supreme authority and our only rule is: Pay the rent each month. We do hold board meetings, but they are really 'ranch' meetings. The board makes the official decisions (based on group consensus rather than majority vote) which the secretary dutifully records. Votes are rarely taken. Furthermore, board decisions are only guide-lines for action. Initiative always comes from individuals. Project is completed only when someone actually wants it enough to carry it out. We have no line-of-command and no police system except group opinion. One of our board members is the 'whip' whose job it is to complain and be troublesome. Another board member is the 'cardinal' who is our conscience and looks out for the consequences of our actions. Our system may seem eccentric and haphazard to those accustomed to regular institutional procedures, but it has evolved organically, and it works for us. When we function well together, it is thrilling to experience our process work through problems. We are continually reaffirming our faith in this process.

I might speculate that anarchy probably works only where each member identifies with the group and feels personally responsible for the whole organization. Conflicts can be acute in this situation, but when they occur in the context of shared common interest, they become vital tensions which maintain a healthy equilibrium. The group definitely has a will of its own, distinct from any individual or sub-group. Our organizational process might best be described as an on-going improvised harmonic piece, based loosely on a traditional form. Not pure anarchy, but not very tightly controlled either.

—Charles Litt

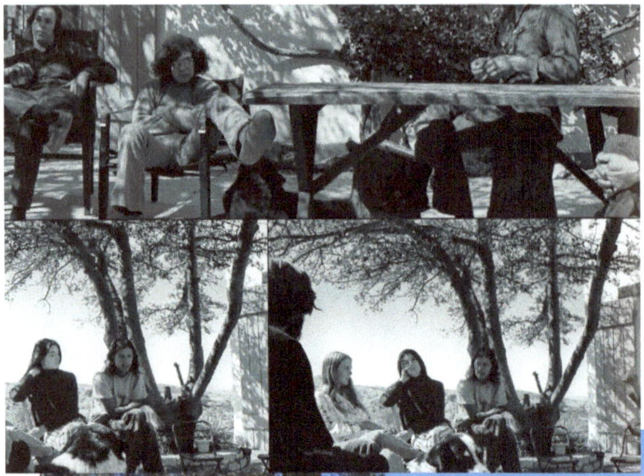

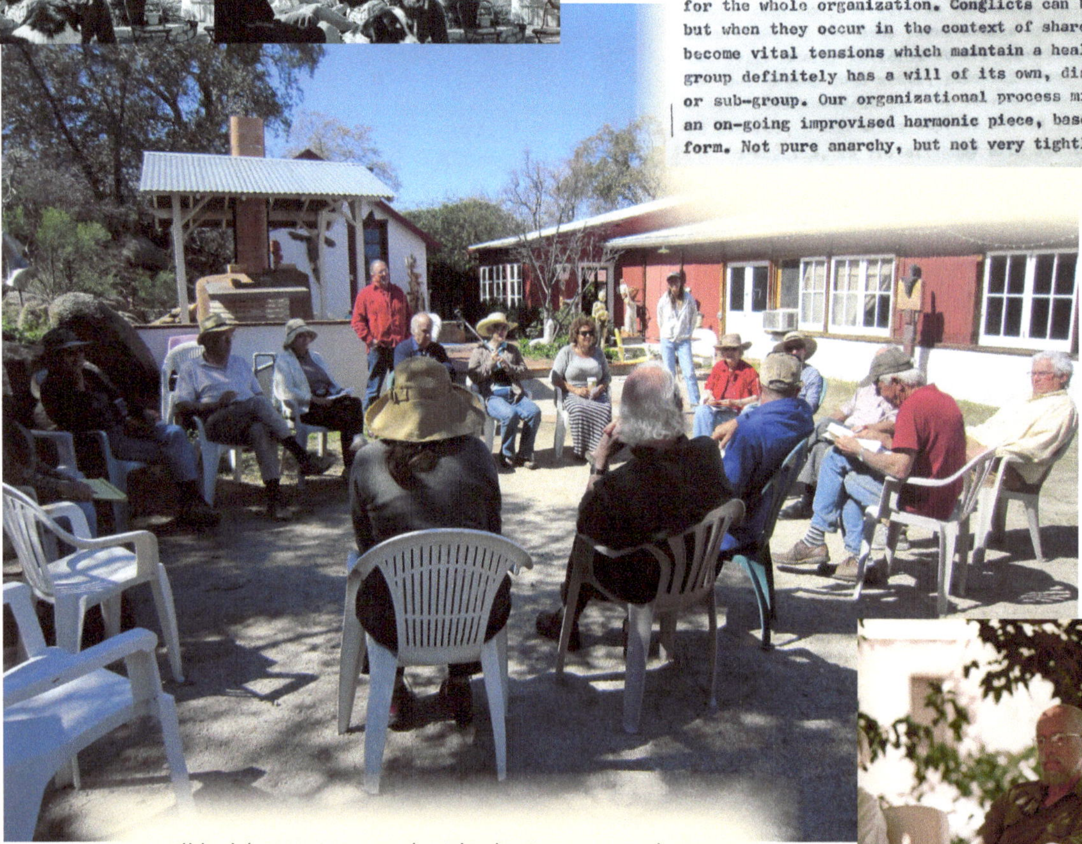

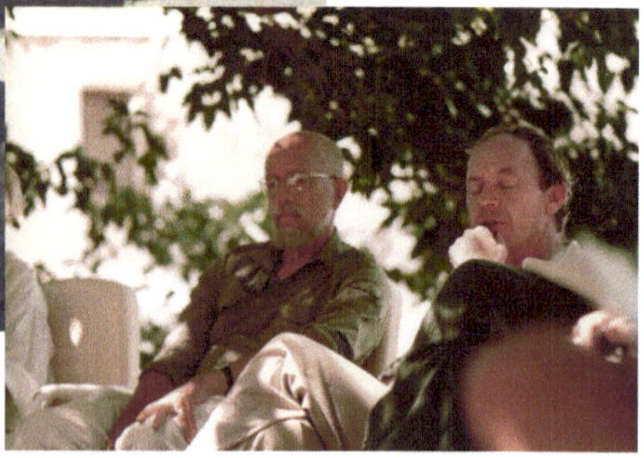

we still hold meetings to decide the important things.
we still talk it up in the road. but nowadays we also
gather opinions through endless chains of email...

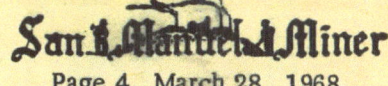

San Manuel Miner

Page 4, March 28, 1968

New Residents Say:

"We are pleased with the reception we have had in Oracle. The friendliness and assistance offered have been generous. We look forward to the future with our new neighbors."

Thanks to our Oracle friends, too many to mention: We love you and appreciate all you've done with and for us over the years. Glad to be part of the life of our town with you!

thanks to all for your loving care of the venerable ranch and its values. We think the present stewardship of the ranch lands and buildings reflects at a very high level the collective/ collaborative principles that our community is based on. It is spiritually and in actuality a very beautiful place! well done all.

love and our continuing support as always

—*stroud and cynthia*

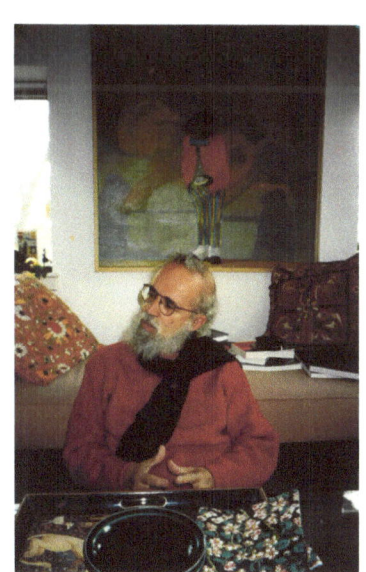

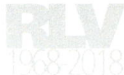

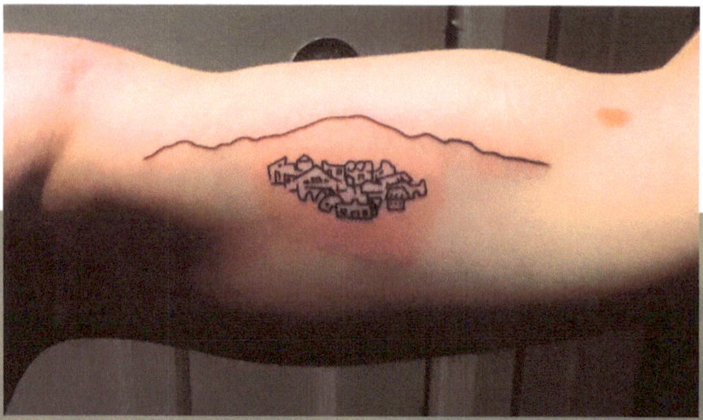

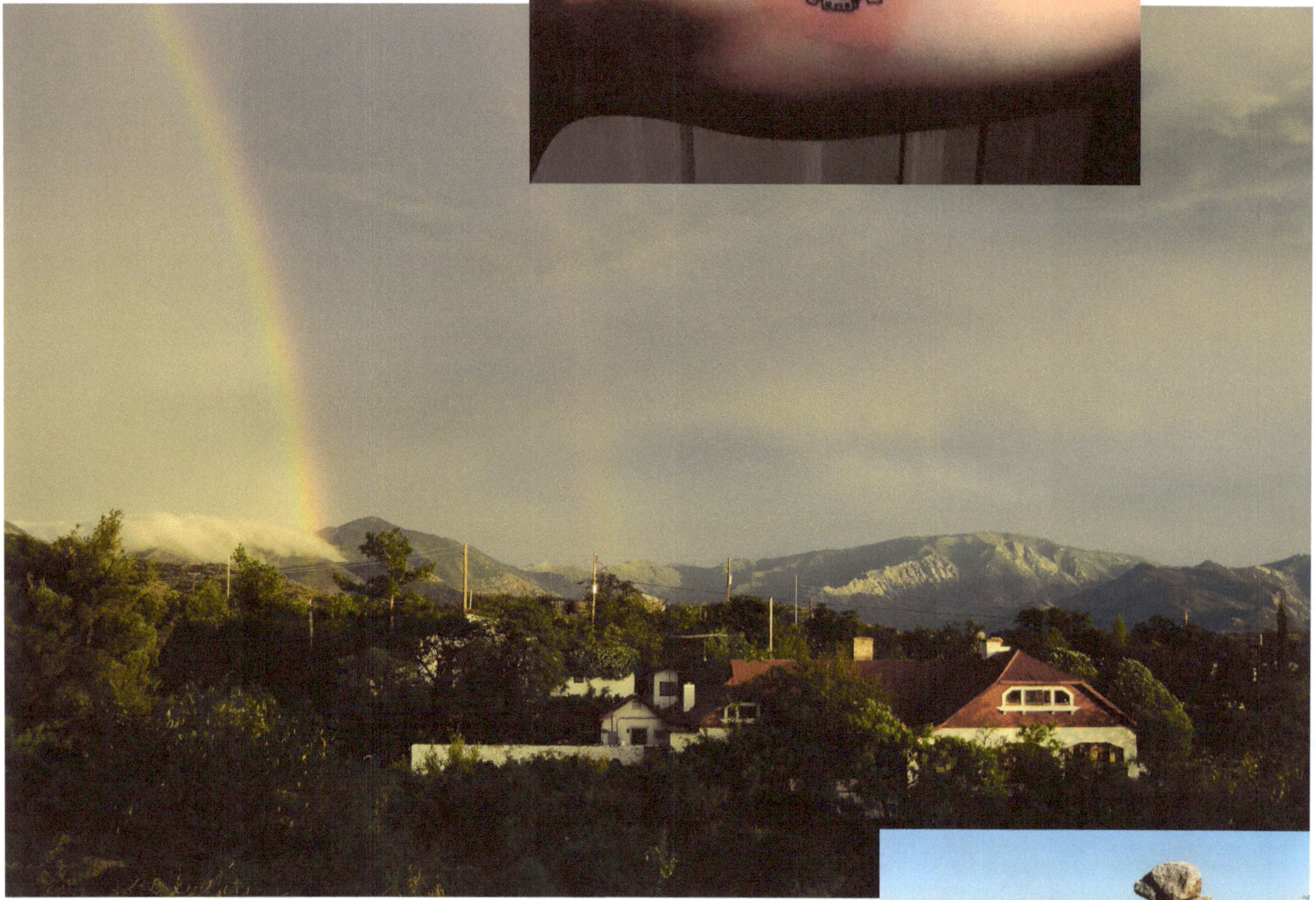

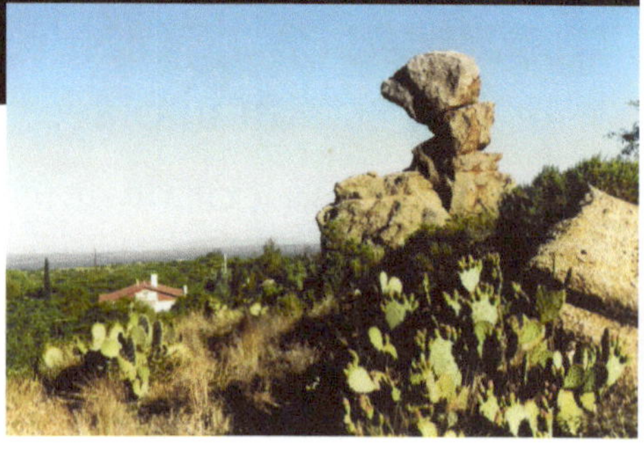

top: Nicolas Baird's tattoo—
original drawing by Charles Littler,
revised by Selina Littler and Nic

www.ingramcontent.com/pod-product-compliance
Lightning Source LLC
Chambersburg PA
CBHW050902180526
45159CB00007B/2759